AUGUSTINE
AND HIS WORLD

·S·AGVSTINVS·

Augustine and His World

Andrew Knowles and Pachomios Penkett

A LION BOOK

For Diane and Philippa

Copyright © 2004 Andrew Knowles and Pachomios Penkett
This edition copyright © 2004 Lion Publishing

The authors assert the moral right
to be identified as the authors of this work

Published by
Lion Publishing plc
Mayfield House, 256 Banbury Road,
Oxford OX2 7DH, England
www.lion-publishing.co.uk
ISBN 0 7459 5104 X

First edition 2004
10 9 8 7 6 5 4 3 2 1 0

All rights reserved

A catalogue record for this book is available
from the British Library

Typeset in 9/12 Modern 880
Printed and bound in China

Contents

Introduction

Augustine is one of the giants of the Christian Church. From his birth in North Africa and his days as a relatively permissive young man, through his midlife conversion to Christianity and career as bishop of Hippo, his story has intrigued and inspired every generation for over 1,600 years.

It is as a thinker, teacher, writer and debater that Augustine's influence has proved most strategic. His greatness lay in his ability to relate the philosophies of Ancient Greece and Rome to the precepts of the Christian faith. Augustine also saved the Church itself from disintegrating into rival factions, by forging sound doctrine in the fires of controversy. Not only did Augustine provide a basis for doctrinal unity, but he presented the Church with a vision for its role in the world. Of all the Christian writers from the earliest centuries down to the present day Augustine is not only one of the most prolific but is also one of the most widely studied, remaining as controversial and influential today as he was during his life.

At the beginning of this third Christian millennium Augustine's fame and fascination are largely due to *City of God* and *Confessions*, his two greatest literary masterpieces. But what of the remaining hundred or so books? And what about the man who wrote them?

In *Augustine and His World* we examine Augustine's life in a series of chapters that look at his adolescence, search for wisdom, conversion, ordination and episcopate. On the way through this life story those influences that most deeply affected Augustine, questions of reason and faith, the interface of pagan philosophy and Christian belief, orthodoxy and heresy, are explored. The final chapter presents aspects of Augustine's significance for subsequent generations.

Augustine also broke new ground in personal spirituality. He probed the depths and recesses of his own heart and mind, memory and motives, to discern the influence of God in his life, and so discovered lessons and insights for every human being. It is not surprising to find, then, that in his own day Augustine was deeply respected not only as a theologian but also as a priest and bishop.

Augustine's ideas are a bridge spanning the gulf between the ancient and medieval worlds, from Aristotle to Anselm. His spiritual quest and ability to express his thoughts reach right to our own day. One prayer in particular that sprang from Augustine's passionate and inquiring soul, 'Our heart is restless until it rests in you', seems to be as pertinent now as it was when it was expressed 16 centuries ago.

As with so much historical study, our work has relied on the research and reflections of many others, and especially on the scholars whose books are listed in the 'Suggestions for Further Reading'. We freely acknowledge our debt to them and hope that new readers will discover their work through this introductory study. The titles of Augustine's writings and their dates are based on *Augustine through the Ages: An Encyclopedia* (General Editor, Allan D. Fitzgerald O.S.A.); and for quotations from *Confessions* we have used Henry Chadwick's excellent translation (Oxford 1991).

Finally, we would like to express our gratitude to Morag Reeve, our commissioning editor at Lion Publishing, and to Jenni Dutton, Laura Derico, Claire Sauer and the design team behind the *Lion Histories* for their skilled work on the text; and to Rosy Baxter, our secretary at Chelmsford Cathedral, who has worked so cheerfully and tirelessly as amanuensis.

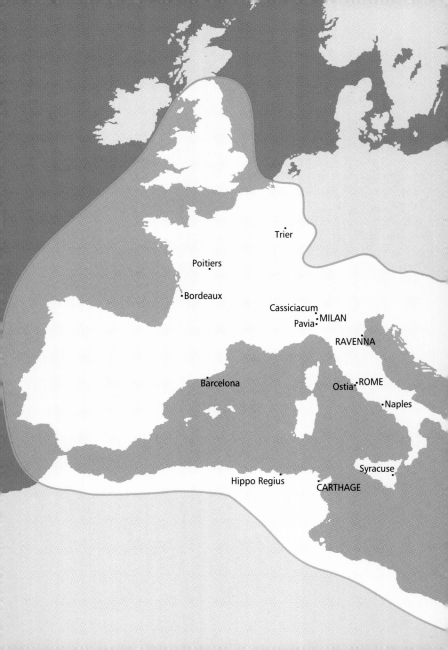

Trier

Poitiers

Bordeaux

Cassiciacum

Pavia •MILAN

RAVENNA

Barcelona

Ostia •ROME

•Naples

Syracuse

Hippo Regius

CARTHAGE

The Roman world at the time of Augustine

—— Boundary of Roman empire

CONSTANTINOPLE
Chalcedon
Philippi
Thessalonica
Nicea
Smyrna
Ephesus
Athens
Antioch
Damascus
Cyrene
Jerusalem
Alexandria

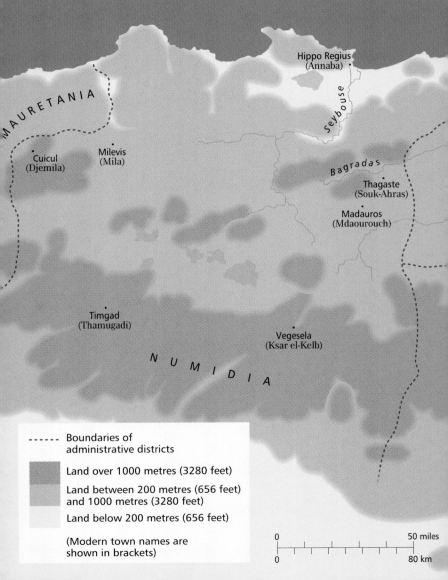

The Roman province of Africa
at the time of Augustine

MAURETANIA

Cuicul
(Djemila)

Milevis
(Mila)

Hippo Regius
(Annaba)

Seybouse

Bagradas

Thagaste
(Souk-Ahras)

Madauros
(Mdaourouch)

Timgad
(Thamugadi)

Vegesela
(Ksar el-Kelb)

N U M I D I A

----- Boundaries of
administrative districts

Land over 1000 metres (3280 feet)

Land between 200 metres (656 feet)
and 1000 metres (3280 feet)

Land below 200 metres (656 feet)

(Modern town names are
shown in brackets)

0   50 miles

0   80 km

Carthage

Medjerda

AFRICA PROCONSULARIS

BYZACENA

Thysdrus
(El Djem)

The World Before Augustine

**The Roman forum
in Rome, Italy,
with the mighty
Colosseum in the
background.**

The province of Africa was an important and
prosperous part of the Roman empire. For the
Romans, Africa was not the vast continent that was
later discovered, but the area that had been controlled by
the main city and sea port of Carthage during the Punic
Wars. Today this area is covered by Tunisia and Western

Libya. The Punic Wars, waged during the third and second centuries before the birth of Christ, were to decide whether Rome or Carthage should control the sea routes and trade of the western Mediterranean. Despite the genius of the Carthaginian leader, Hannibal, who sprang a surprise attack on Rome by crossing the Alps with elephants, the Romans won the wars and destroyed Carthage in 146 BC.

Roman rule

In the middle of the fourth century AD, the Roman empire had reached the summit of its extent and influence. Its territory extended from Hadrian's Wall, in northern Britain, to Antioch and the eastern provinces, some 3,000 miles from Rome. The north-eastern frontier lay between Germany and barbarian tribes: Goths, Huns and Vandals. To the south, with its seaboard on the Mediterranean, was the province of Africa. It is here, in a town called Thagaste, that Augustine was born on AD 13 November 354.

In theory the Roman empire was a realm of peace, justice and prosperity, founded on Roman law and protected by the Roman army. But the military were overextended in maintaining such long frontiers, and barbarian tribes were pressing on the borders. Security was costly in money and recruits, so that treaties, alliances and compromises had to be made with real or potential enemies. Some barbarian tribes were enlisted as Roman auxiliaries and became as well armed and war wise as the Romans themselves. From time to time, the army commanders themselves attempted to seize power, both in Italy and in the provinces, and it was a period of almost continuous civil war. Meanwhile, the Roman upper class had become complacent and self-indulgent – preoccupied with personal status and political infighting. In short, the peak of Roman supremacy was also the cusp of decline.

Augustine's life would span the decline and fall of the Roman empire. On New Year's Eve 406, a horde of Goths, Huns and Vandals would cross the frozen Rhine to sweep into Gaul and then across the Pyrenees into Spain. In 410, Rome itself would be overwhelmed and sacked by the forces of Alaric the Goth.

Meanwhile, speed of communication was one of the wonders of the Roman world. Straight roads and safe seaways (at least in the summer months), together with the common language of Latin, meant that news and instructions could travel rapidly between the centre of the empire and its provinces. But the emperors were not always at the centre and the centre was not always at Rome. The fastest communication was at the pace of a galloping horse, with riders delivering letters by relay through a series of posting stations. But armies of infantry could manoeuvre no faster than marching

Carthage imagined at the height of its power, nineteenth-century engraving, Bibliothèque des Arts Decoratifs, Paris.

sandals and aching legs would allow. 'Rapid response' to barbarian incursions or local riots could take several months. So it was that when Emperor Theodosius I died in AD 395, this vast but unwieldy empire was divided between his two sons, Honorius in the west and Arcadius in the east. The capital of the western empire continued to be Rome, although the administrative centre might be elsewhere. The capital of the eastern empire was Constantinople.

Communication between Rome and North Africa was relatively simple, with a summer sea voyage from Rome's port of Ostia bringing passengers to Carthage in a matter of days. Augustine would be both a student and a teacher in Carthage, and the voyages to Ostia and back (albeit five years apart) would be the only sea journeys of his life.

When the Romans conquered Carthage, they took over the Phoenician cities along the mediterranean coast and developed the towns of the inland plateau. They linked them by roads and bridges to one another and the sea ports, and improved the water supply by building

The coastline of North Africa, where Morocco borders the Mediterranean Sea.

aqueducts, reservoirs and cisterns. As a result, the province of Africa entered an era of unparalleled prosperity, with towns and rural estates alike thriving on commerce and agriculture.

The capital, Carthage, was developed by successive Roman emperors. Augustus, who was the first emperor (from 14 BC to AD 27) levelled the Byrsa – the high point overlooking the city – and built an esplanade. Hadrian (emperor from AD 117 to 138) constructed an aqueduct 80 miles long to supply the city with millions of gallons of water. His successor, Antoninus, completed the huge baths and a massive basilica. There was a grand amphitheatre, the largest circus outside Rome, and a fine palace for the proconsul. Carthage became the second city of the western Roman empire.

From Carthage, merchants traded throughout the known world. The export of cereal crops made North Africa the breadbasket of the empire, and especially of Rome. The region produced olives and olive oil in huge quantities, red-slip tableware, and marble of a quality for monumental buildings. Hadrian quarried marble from Africa for his Pantheon in Rome, transporting 50-foot columns over high mountains to the port of Thabraca. During this period of peace and prosperity, educated people built comfortable villas, which they decorated with exquisite mosaics.

This stone figure, perhaps depicting a nature god, once marked a grave in ancient Carthage.

Inland, peasant farmers lived in ancient, close-knit communities: the Berber or Carthaginian underclass that had no stake in Roman colonialism. They maintained their Punic cults and language, although in time their fertility gods became identified with the gods and goddesses of Greece and Rome: 'Baal-Hammon' with Saturn, god of time and harvest, and 'Tanit' with Juno, goddess of marriage. But even those who resisted Roman ways could still make their living by growing corn and olives for Italy. Vast olive groves stretched 50 miles further south than their cultivation line today, as the remains of olive presses and the ruins of fine buildings testify. At remote El Djem was a venue to seat 30,000 people: the amphitheatre of Roman Thysdrus, which for a time supplanted Carthage.

A Roman legion was based in Africa for internal security and to help with engineering and agricultural projects. There was also a cohort on duty in Carthage. But the soldiers who assisted with the construction of roads and irrigation could be heavy handed in matters of law and order, and the army presence was an aggravation. The military seized land on which nomadic tribes had for centuries grazed their cattle, causing resentment and outbreaks of violence. They also used indigenous people as migrant labour at harvest time, requiring them by law to give six days' work per year in return for squatters' rights. They often required them to work more, which was another cause of unrest.

The most fertile land was the valley of the Medjerda, where Augustine was born. Much of it was under imperial administration, having been confiscated from senators by Emperor Nero (emperor from AD 54 to 68). Now Roman methods of cultivation and the planting of endless acres of olive groves had altered the terrain. And the ancient towns, with their houses cut into the rock, had acquired arched gates, paved streets, market squares with cisterns and forums with statues. The Romans had come to stay.

Whatever the friction, the Romans were good for Africa. It was not only the land and the towns but the people who had the chance to develop, gain an education and make their way both locally and in the wider empire. Augustine chose this door of opportunity, and was by no means the only African to do so. These were exciting times of mobility and adventure for people from humble backgrounds, with careers in the army or the civil service, which could lead anywhere from Asia to Britain and result in honour, wealth and influence.

'May I have joy of the beasts that are prepared for me. I pray too that they may prove prompt with me. I will entice them to devour me quickly… if only I reach Jesus Christ.'

IGNATIUS, BISHOP OF ANTIOCH, C. 35–107

Early Christianity

And what of the Church? Three centuries had passed since the life, death and resurrection of Jesus Christ. By the time Augustine was born, in AD 354, Christianity had developed from a novel Jewish cult to a way of life followed by many throughout the empire, east and west. The leading apostles of the Church, Peter and Paul, had recognized that the new faith must break out of its Jewish context to engage with all nations and cultures. The first generation, with this missionary vision, saw the Christian gospel preached and churches planted in such significant centres as Antioch, Ephesus, Philippi – and Rome.

'Surely I am coming soon. Amen. Come, Lord Jesus.'

REVELATION 22:20

The early Christians hoped that Jesus Christ would return in their lifetime; an expectation that shines out from the Gospels and Paul's letters. Christ's 'second coming' would vindicate his suffering followers and establish the kingdom of God. In the meantime, life was a struggle between good and evil; but it was a battle that Jesus had already won through his sacrificial death and resurrection. Now the task of his Church was to live with purity and integrity in the 'last days' before God's final judgment. These end times were characterized by human stress, natural disasters and religious persecution – all of which were fulfilled many times over in the unfolding history of the Roman empire.

Christ depicted as
a sun god. Early
Christian
ceramic.

Jesus did not return, and Christians were persecuted, imprisoned and martyred for their faith. Some survived in secret fellowships like

*'If anyone denies
that he is a
Christian, and
proves it in
practice by
worshipping our
gods, he shall be
pardoned.'*

EMPEROR TRAJAN IN
A LETTER TO PLINY
THE YOUNGER, C. 112

**Christ encounters
the Samaritan
woman at the
well. Wall painting
in the Via Latina
Catacomb, Rome
(c. 260–320).**

those of the catacombs in Rome, but others met their deaths as sport for the bloodthirsty audiences in the amphitheatres. Christians were law-abiding citizens in every way, except that they refused to sacrifice to idols or worship 'the genius of the emperor'. They openly criticized the sacrificial rites that were used to promote social cohesion or honour the emperor as divine. Like the Jews before them, they acknowledged only one God, whom they held was fully revealed in his Son, Jesus Christ.

Christian customs

The title 'Christian' had begun as a nickname for those who aspired to be 'like Christ'. They met to 'break bread' in their homes, perhaps on the 'Lord's Day', which was Sunday, the day of the resurrection of Jesus and the first day of the week. They shared a communal meal, known as the *agape* or love feast, which took place in an evening and to which everyone was welcome, rich and poor alike. The

'breaking of bread', however, was different from a meal, in that it formally re-enacted the action of Jesus at the last supper and soon became the more stylized Eucharist (thanksgiving). The early Christians initiated new members by baptism in water after careful and sometimes lengthy instruction.

The Church's worship followed an annual cycle. The central event was Easter, which was preceded by 'Lent': a 40-day period reflecting the time of Jesus' temptation in the wilderness. The historical events of Christ's birth and baptism were commemorated, and well-known martyrs such as John the Baptist, Stephen, Peter and Paul were remembered. Gradually these special days were integrated into the liturgical year.

In addition to the scriptures, there was a short manual of Christian teaching, known as the *Didache*, or *The Teaching of the Lord Through the Twelve Apostles*. It was discovered in Constantinople in 1873 and probably came from Smyrna (modern Izmir). There were also letters from bishops such as Clement of Rome (c. AD 96) and Ignatius of Antioch (c. 35–c. 107). These give glimpses of the issues and activities of the churches in the first century. The bishops' concerns were for the unity of the Church in the celebration of the Eucharist, for appropriate discipline and properly authorized leadership.

The first century of Christianity saw the Church's mission expand from Jerusalem to Rome. The second century (between 150 and 250) saw the Church facing a series of challenges and potential setbacks. From outside, Christians were persecuted, imprisoned and martyred for their faith. From within, differences of belief and practice led to divisions and the formation of 'sects'. Inevitably, the Church became preoccupied with formulating its core convictions, not least to determine which 'sects' were orthodox ('right') and which were heretical ('wrong'). This period also saw the birth of monasticism, which would grow at a spectacular rate and replace martyrdom as an expression of 'dying to self in order to live to God'.

'This food is called the Eucharist, and of it no one is allowed to partake but he who believes that our teachings are true, and has been washed with the washing for the remission of sins and unto regeneration, and who also lives as Christ directed.'

JUSTIN, C. 150

'On Sunday, the Lord's own day, come together, break bread and carry out the eucharist, first confessing your sins so that your offering may be pure.'

DIDACHE 14.1

Important theologians appeared in these early centuries. Later known as the Church Fathers, they helped to establish church teaching and to protect Christianity from heresies such as Gnosticism. These early figures include Irenaeus, Tertullian, Origen, Clement of Alexandria and Cyprian of Carthage. They sought to elucidate orthodox teaching on questions such as the true nature of Christ, the meaning of salvation and the interpretation of scripture. Augustine was not the first Church Father; he followed in a line of brilliant theologians and was, as we shall see, considerably influenced by those who preceded him.

The Roman authorities were suspicious of the Church. The refusal of Christians to worship the old gods was seen as dangerous, because therein lay protection and prosperity. And to deny the supreme authority of the emperor was treason. But Christians had 'another King' in Jesus, and he alone was the Lord who commanded their worship. So Christians were considered to be atheists and their religion 'illicit' or unlicensed. They were also suspected of cannibalism (because they spoke of 'eating flesh' and 'drinking blood') and immorality (because of their 'love feasts').

Persecutions give way to peace

The persecutions of early centuries gave way to a period of relative peace at the start of the fourth century. In 306 a new emperor was proclaimed in York. His name was Constantine, and he was to rule from 306 to 337. One of his lasting achievements was to found the city of Constantinople, which was named after him, and which became the eastern capital of the empire in AD 395. But it was Constantine's conversion through a vision before the Battle of Milvian Bridge, near Rome, in 312, that was to have undreamed-of significance. At the moment he established his authority to rule, by defeating the pagans under Maxentius, Constantine became a devoted Christian and an enormously influential protector and patron of the Church.

In 313, Constantine inaugurated a policy of religious freedom. Christians were allowed to worship freely and all their property was restored that had been confiscated or destroyed in the persecution since 303. Constantine wanted to unite the Christian Church to the empire and concerned himself with the issues that divided the Church. He summoned councils, going to great lengths to ensure that bishops could attend from all over the empire; but he did not control the Church in any legal way, nor was he its constitutional head.

A contemporary bust (c. 280) of Emperor Constantine I.

Constantine showed an ongoing commitment to Christian principles. The first Christian symbols appeared on the coinage in 315, and the judgments of ecclesiastical courts became recognized by the State. He reformed the laws on debt and the conditions of slaves, supported the poor and freed celibates and unmarried people from special taxation. In 321 he ordered that Sunday should be observed as a public holiday and generously endowed church building projects in Constantinople, Palestine and Rome. The basilica style of church became commonplace, with 40 in Rome alone.

Under Constantine's influence and patronage, bishops became public figures and the Church an institution of wealth and influence. The Church was allowed to inherit property and so began to consolidate power and wield patronage in its own right. By the end of the fourth and the beginning of the fifth century, bishops such as Ambrose at Milan and Paulinus at Nola were a force to be reckoned with in their respective communities, able to play power politics with the secular authorities. Ambrose was an eloquent preacher in Latin who had a considerable and effective following in Milan – enough to confront the imperial power that was then based in the same city.

At Antioch, John Chrysostom wielded enormous influence, although he was not at that time a bishop.

'All judges, city-people and craftsmen shall rest on the venerable day of the Sun. But countrymen may without hindrance attend to agriculture, since it often happens that this is the most suitable day for sowing grain or planting vines.'

CONSTANTINE'S
LEGISLATION FOR
THE OBSERVANCE OF
SUNDAY, 321

His name, meaning 'golden mouth', was earned by the magnificent eloquence with which he stirred Christians to resist the abuses of Roman government. He became bishop of Constantinople in 397 but was exiled in 403 by the empress Eudoxia for denouncing her as a 'Jezebel'.

It must not, though, be assumed that from Constantine onwards Christianity was a runaway success. Persecution had ended and the Church was allowed some economic advantage and political opportunity. Much depended on the personality of the emperor and the quality of the bishops. The court of Theodosius II (eastern emperor from AD 408 to 450) was so predominantly Christian that some said it resembled a convent. By the early fifth century it was fashionable among the Roman aristocracy to be Christian and attitudes finally shifted from throwing believers to lions to helping them build churches. But pagan beliefs and practices were a long time dying, and even in the middle of the fifth century, Pope Leo the Great (pope from 440 to 460) had to take

Monasticism

The monastic movement grew rapidly from the late third century onwards; the name 'monk' (from the Greek *monachos*) meaning 'one who is alone'. Individuals withdrew to the desert to live a solitary life of prayer, visiting one another or gathering occasionally. The most celebrated hermit was Antony of Egypt (d. AD 356), who gave spiritual counsel to visitors and about whom many inspiring stories were told. A *Life of Antony* was translated from Greek into Latin by Jerome and became immensely popular among upper-class Romans. Meanwhile, Pachomios (d. AD 346) at Tabennisi in Upper Egypt, pioneered a rule by which monks could live together in community. He was a founding father of monasticism.

issue with his congregation for bowing to the sun before entering St Peter's in Rome.

But by the time of Augustine things had certainly greatly improved for the Christian Church. He was to enter a world of fierce debate and controversy, yet also one of relative peace.

C H A P T E R   2

The Young Man

Aurelius Augustinus – to be known to the world as Augustine – was born in North Africa on AD 13 November 354, in a Roman-style town 200 miles from the sea and 2,000 feet above it. In those days the place was called Thagaste, but today it is the town of Souk-Ahras in Algeria. The wider region was known as Numidia, after the Roman word for 'nomads'.

'To praise you is the desire of man, a little piece of your creation.'

CONFESSIONS 1.1.1

A Roman town

In Thagaste there were people of several races and religions. The original Berber population had mixed and interbred with the peoples who had conquered or done business with them: Phoenicians, Romans, Greeks and Jews. The region was also popular with veteran soldiers retiring from imperial service, many of whom settled in North Africa and married local women. But the truth was that the line of 'civilization' ran between the Romans and the rest. Augustine may never have spoken any language but

Latin, and all other dialects he grouped under the general term 'Punic'.

The wealthier inhabitants of the town had a strong loyalty to Roman government and Roman lifestyle. They knew and used Latin and lived by the law and order, self-discipline and public service that had made Rome great. In their integrity and high moral values, they were probably more 'Roman' than the Romans, because in some parts of the empire the old order was starting to crumble. Thagaste's public buildings included baths, temples and amphitheatres. The baths were the social

Vestiges of the Roman empire in arch and pillars at the site of Roman Volubilis, Morocco.

centres of the day, while the theatres were the venues for drama, oratory, games and spectacles. Well-to-do estate owners had villas in the surrounding countryside, where they lived in comfort off the land and the labour of exploited peasants. These peasants were poor and marginalized, but armed with a vigorous form of Christianity, which gave them courage and hope in their troubles.

Thagaste

The modern town of Souk-Ahras stands on the border between Algeria and Tunisia. In the nineteenth century it was a French colonial settlement, with a main square and bandstand. Flaubert, in 1858, found it 'atrocious, cold and muddy'. In the twentieth century the working of the mines and the arrival of the railway brought the town some significance and prosperity.

In the distant past, and long before the Romans came, Souk-Ahras was the Numidian town of Thagaste: set in the valley of Medjerda on the uplands of north-east Numidia, and watered by the Bagradas river. The altitude and rainfall were similar to Madrid today: dry and hot in summer, with an uncomfortable sirocco wind. To the east were mountains rising to a height of 3,000 feet.

In Roman times, the people of Thagaste worked the fertile soil to produce corn and olives. In the surrounding hills and forests they snared wild animals such as lions, bears and panthers, to be sent for sport in the amphitheatres of Carthage or Rome.

In Souk-Ahras today, the church is named after the town's most famous son, Augustine; and in the crypt is a small museum dedicated to his memory.

A pagan father...

Augustine's father was Patricius, a well-respected member of the town. He was a proud man, holding the office of *decurio*, or town councillor; but he was poor. Augustine describes his father's estate as 'a few acres'. As a leading member of the community, Patricius was expected to support public services and sports with his own money. Many councillors were reduced to poverty in this way and Patricius himself may have fallen on hard times. However, the family were fortunate in having a relative who was willing to help them: Romanianus, a wealthy estate owner and local celebrity. It is he who funded the classical education that unlocked the doors of opportunity for Augustine, and also became his close friend.

... and a Christian mother

Augustine's mother was Monica. She had been married at the age of 12 but was 23 by the time Augustine was born. She had another son, Navigius, and one or two daughters; but it is because of her devotion to Augustine that she became immortalized. Her name is of Berber origin, from a local goddess, 'Mon'. The Berbers were a fair-skinned and fair-haired people who lived in North Africa long before the arrival of the Phoenicians or the Romans. The Romans nicknamed them 'Barbarians' and mimicked their speech as a primitive 'burr-burr'.

When they were first married, Monica had lived with Patricius in his mother's house. Her relationship with her mother-in-law had been difficult at first, because the servants told tales against her. But the young wife had won through with patience and respect. Over the years she was a faithful and loving wife to Patricius, despite his hot tempers and many affairs. And Patricius became a Christian before he died.

Patricius and Monica agreed that their gifted son should have a classical education. Such an education would be expensive and require them to make considerable

'I was already a believer, as were my mother and the entire household, except for my father... [My mother] anxiously laboured to convince me that you, my God, were my father rather than he.'

CONFESSIONS 1.11.17

sacrifices; but it would lay the foundation for a prosperous and perhaps even distinguished career in the Roman civil service. The unusual name they gave their son – 'Augustine', meaning 'little emperor' – signalled their shared ambition.

Darkness and light

In Africa, the native religions were pagan and deeply superstitious. The Berbers worshipped the spirits of the dead and warded off evil with magic charms. The Phoenicians engaged in occult ceremonies, using

Monica

Monica was a deeply committed Christian with a strict and somewhat superstitious faith. She observed, for example, the local practice of keeping sabbath fasts, and the very widespread custom of sharing meals with the dead by holding picnics and parties at their tombs. For Christians, death was a birthday and the anniversary was celebrated as such. When Monica attempted to take a basket of refreshments to a grave in Milan, she was told that the bishop there, Ambrose, had forbidden it. Monica also believed in divine guidance and paid close attention to dreams as messages from another world.

Monica had received a careful Christian upbringing and wanted the same for her children. She was determined, even controlling, but also affectionate and intelligent. Augustine became the focal point of her life, and she dedicated 20 years of prayers and tears to the cause of him becoming a Christian. As a young man, Augustine's respect for his mother was never in doubt, but his independent spirit chafed against her possessiveness and ambition. In his late twenties, Augustine actually left Monica in Carthage and sailed for Rome without saying goodbye. In her determination she followed him to Rome and went with him to Milan, where she became a much-appreciated member of his household, and shared with him an extraordinary vision of bliss before her death.

sacrifices in their attempts to appease the gods and control the forces of nature. Carthage was a major centre for the worship of the Baal fertility gods, Hammon and his consort Tanit, who in extreme circumstances were offered human victims.

Into this sombre and fearful world, Christianity brought the good news of one all-powerful invisible and loving creator God, and a Saviour who could defeat every kind of evil. But the Christians were seen as a threat to the old ways and vested interests, and were persecuted as a result. Emperor Decius (249–51) suppressed the

'She had brought up her children, enduring travail as she saw them wandering away from you... She exercised care for everybody as if they were all her own children.'

AUGUSTINE ABOUT HIS MOTHER, *CONFESSIONS* 9.9.22

Augustine and his mother, Monica, share their vision at Ostia shortly before her death. A popular picture by Ary Scheffer (1854), National Gallery, London.

Early learning

When he was about 43 and a bishop in Hippo, Augustine told the story of his life in his *Confessions*. He remembered, or at least reflected on, his early years; the process of learning language as an infant, and the anger and jealousy that is inherent in human nature from babyhood: 'The feebleness of infant limbs is innocent, not the infant's mind. I have personally watched and studied a jealous baby' (*Confessions* 1.7.11).

He was intrigued by the stages of human development and the relationship between thought and will and action.

Christians with great brutality, requiring them to offer sacrifices to the ancient gods of Rome. Many African Christians, to save their lives or property, betrayed their faith by handing over their copies of the scriptures and other holy books to the secular authorities. Some of those who refused to compromise were imprisoned or killed. From these contrasting responses sprang a long-running division in the African Church, between the 'Catholic' compromisers and the faithful martyrs, later known as 'Donatists'.

Religion and politics were interwoven. Couples like Patricius and Monica saw themselves as superior to the local Numidian peasants. They expressed this in their allegiance to Rome and (in Monica's case) to Catholic Christianity. For them, Rome meant protection and prosperity. Monica's family were Catholic Christians who followed the inclusive approach of Bishop Cyprian, but were regarded as 'worldly' by the more exclusive and hard-line Church of the martyrs and 'confessors'. The common people, including many Numidians, found the Church of the martyrs more popular and exciting. Their numbers grew as the power of Rome and the influence of the Catholic Church began to fade.

Paganism was in decline around the empire, not least because Christianity was giving a sense of value to every human being, irrespective of class, wealth or education. By the time Augustine was in his thirties, imperial edicts were being issued to suppress paganism, ordering idols to be destroyed and temples closed. But Augustine very fairly observed that he knew pagans who lived better lives than he did.

Augustine was not baptized as a baby, but rather welcomed into the Christian Church with a blessing, the sign of the cross and a touch of salt. As he grew, he would have gone with his mother to church. Baptism was delayed

'The free-ranging flux of curiosity is channelled by discipline under your laws, God.'

CONFESSIONS 1.14.23

A divided Church

One of the great 'Fathers' of the African Church, Tertullian, had taught that there was no way back to the Church for those who had betrayed Christ. He had denounced the Catholics for their compromises and himself joined a vigorous and highly spiritual sect called the Montanists.

However, when the Decian persecution came to North Africa, there were some Catholic Christians who suffered for their faith and survived. These were the 'confessors', whose courage and faithfulness might outweigh the failings of the rest. Cyprian, the bishop of Carthage, certainly saw it that way.

Tertullian (c. 160–220), 'the Latin Father of the Church', lived in Carthage. He wrote brilliant and ironic defences of Christianity. Engraving by Étienne Gautier (1842–1903).

By the time Augustine was born in 354, a deep split had developed between those Christians who followed Cyprian, living under the authority of the Catholic Church, and those who became known as 'Donatists', whose faith was a pure, spiritual commitment, unsullied by compromise with a worldly institution.

until late in life, to increase the chances of a sinless death; but when Augustine contracted a childhood illness that appeared life-threatening, preparations were made for an emergency baptism. In the event, he made a speedy recovery, and would not be baptized until Easter 387 when he was over 30.

Schooling at Thagaste

Augustine's early schooling was in Thagaste. As a boy, he learned to read and write, loving Latin, but hating Greek.

Cyprian
(c. 200–58),
bishop of
Carthage,
brought before
Emperor Valerian
(r. 253–60). A
Spanish painting
from Catalonia,
fourteenth
century.

By his own account, he preferred games to books and was often in trouble with his teachers. He likened the lessons to the labour and sorrow of Adam, and his beatings to the sufferings of the Christian martyrs.

His early prayers included fervent pleas to be spared the rod: 'Though I was only a small child, there was great feeling when I pleaded with you that I might not be caned at school' (*Confessions* 1.9.14).

In *City of God*, Augustine wrote: 'Who would not choose death to beginning childhood all over again?'

Cyprian takes a stand

Next to Augustine, Cyprian of Carthage (d. 258) is the most important bishop in the history of North Africa. He was reluctant to permanently excommunicate those Christians who had lapsed in the face of persecution. He required only that they do penance or wait a certain time before being reinstated. But in Rome, a rigorist by the name of Novatian was attacking his bishop, Cornelius (d. 253), for being too lenient. When Novatian sought an ally in Cyprian, he was rebuffed, the bishop of Carthage preferring restoration to condemnation in the case of his weaker brethren.

Cyprian found support for a policy of rebaptizing those who had split from the Church but now wanted to return. His fellow African bishops agreed that this reduced the risk of independent groups forming to administer the sacraments outside the authority of the Catholic Church. For Cyprian, the sacraments were not efficacious outside the Church, because the Church alone was the body of Christ in which the Holy Spirit resided. It followed that no one outside the Church was authorized to administer the sacraments. This stance led to a rift between Cyprian and Cornelius's successor, Stephen, who had taken much tougher measures to punish schismatics.

'I was next sent to school to learn to read and write. Poor wretch, I did not understand for what such knowledge is useful. Yet if ever I was indolent in learning, I was beaten.'

CONFESSIONS 1.9.14

Augustine's failure to master Greek was a great disadvantage to him in later life. Greek was the language of the eastern empire and accomplished scholars would be bilingual, as Cicero had been. Although Augustine would have known some Greek, he was never fluent, which meant that his reading of Greek philosophy was always 'second-hand' through translations.

Augustine was, in fact, a gifted and promising pupil. He developed a love of the theatre, Latin literature and 'rhetoric' – the use of language. The mark of the cultured person was an ability to conjure words and phrases, puns and rhymes, metaphors and irony. Augustine was to have this ability in abundance, and it would pour from him in a lifetime of conversation, debate, letters and sermons. At this stage, his own ambition was to become a schoolmaster himself, but Patricius hoped his son would qualify as a lawyer or rhetorician. At the age of 11, it was decided to send Augustine to a better school for the next stage of his education.

'Words are like exquisite and precious vessels.'

CONFESSIONS 1.16.26

Schooling at Madauros

Augustine's new school was at Madauros (modern-day Mdaourouch), a small Numidian city about 19 miles, a day's journey, to the south of Thagaste. Madauros was a university town, larger and more pagan than Thagaste, with two statues of Mars, the Roman god of war, prominent in its centre. One of Africa's famous writers came from here: Lucius Apuleius (c. 125–after 170), an eccentric philosopher whose novel *The Golden Ass* was a scandalous adventure of myth, magic and sex. Augustine became accustomed to the sight of revellers staggering home from their drunken Bacchanals.

At Madauros, the emphasis of Augustine's education was on the rules of language and the structure of persuasive argument. The method was very traditional, rigorous and tedious, aiming to develop a perfect, precise understanding of the meanings and use of words by studying the works of classical Latin writers. He learned by heart extracts of the great Roman orator Cicero (106–43 BC), and was taught the principles of oratory and debate. Here were laid the foundations for Augustine's own speaking, writing and preaching in years to come, and not least in learning how to appeal to the emotions.

A waning empire

During Augustine's early years, the glory of the Roman empire was, almost imperceptibly, on the wane. The discipline and dedication of the Roman way of life was giving way to a greater flamboyance of dress, extravagance of lifestyle and specious spirituality. Successive emperors were preoccupied with the defence of their territories against barbarian insurgents from the north and the military threat of Persia in the east. Their centre of government was no longer Rome, but Trier, or Milan, or Ravenna, as they moved with their armies between Gaul, northern Italy and the Danube. Although there was a revival of interest in literature, the main concern was for the might and muscle to preserve the empire at all. Imperial control in the western empire was exercised through crippling levels of taxation and a brutal enforcement of the law.

In these days of slow decline, there was little need for the talents of the North Africans, who were almost old-fashioned in their provincial Roman ways. Although, since Constantine, there was optimism that the Roman empire and the Christian Church would rule the world for ever, a very different underlying trend was revealed in the careers of Augustine and his contemporaries. Many of them, like Augustine, returned to North Africa and their small home towns; some of them eventually becoming bishops. Augustine himself, after standing on the threshold of a distinguished career in Milan, came full circle to Thagaste to settle for the obscurity of a monastic community in his family home.

'Clouds of
muddy carnal
concupiscence
filled the air. The
bubbling
impulses of
puberty befogged
and obscured my
heart.'

CONFESSIONS 2.2.2

*'All around me
hissed a
cauldron of illicit
loves.'*

CONFESSIONS 3.1.1

'Eat, drink and
be merry.' A
Roman banquet
portrayed in a
first-century
fresco found at
Pompeii. National
Museum of
Archaeology,
Naples.

In addition to Cicero, Augustine encountered the works of Terence and Virgil, Ovid, Seneca and Juvenal. He delighted in the great Latin literature, which moved him to tears on occasion, and he learned to emulate its persuasive skills. He won a prize for his rendition of a famous scene from Virgil, in which Dido, the queen of Carthage, first pours out her grief and then takes her own life as her lover Aeneas sails away to his destiny and the founding of Rome. The class erupted in applause.

Loose living

When Augustine was about 15 years old, his parents decided to send him to university at Carthage. It took them a year to raise the necessary money, and during this time Augustine was at home in Thagaste. Without a school to attend, and brimming with adolescent energy, he became part of a group of lads who ran wild in the town, proud of their exploits at drinking, theft and sex. For the son of a devout Christian mother, this was the start of a long struggle against the lure of paganism. Perhaps Augustine's famous prayer, 'Grant me chastity and continence, but not yet' (*Confessions* 8.7.17), was born from the conflict of his upbringing, between his mother's piety and his father's permissiveness.

*'Shame for its
own sake.'*

CONFESSIONS 2.4.9

Shameful memories

In his *Confessions*, Augustine recalled some events from his adolescent years. He remembered the sense of shame when his father caught sight of him naked at the baths. In Roman times there was nothing untoward about nakedness, but clearly there was some embarrassment between father and son. As Patricius smiled knowingly at Augustine's evident emergence into manhood, the young man felt himself exposed and ashamed. In his mind he associated the episode with the story of Adam and Eve, with its suggestive juxtaposition of nakedness and guilt.

On another occasion, the teenage Augustine and his friends stole some pears. They weren't hungry and soon threw them away, but the prank stuck in Augustine's mind as an example of sin. Again, the story of Adam and Eve had centred on fruit stolen from the Garden of Eden. As a bishop, Augustine searched his heart for the motives of such an act. Partly they had desired something beautiful that belonged to someone else. But there was also peer pressure. He would never have stolen the pears without the encouragement of a gang of friends. In the group, he would 'have been ashamed not to be shameless' (*Confessions* 2.9.17). So here was an irony: that two of God's good gifts, the love of beautiful objects and the joy of friendship, could motivate a furtive, pointless and guilt-producing act of theft.

Wrestling with evil

At the end of his teenage years, as a student in Carthage, Augustine became a Manichee. The Manichaean sect was a distortion of Christianity that believed evil was a tangible power to be wrestled with and rejected. But Augustine, on reflection, concluded that evil was a distortion of good. For example, friendship was good. The same power of friendship that had motivated the theft of the pears would be the force that held him in the fellowship of the Manichees long after he ceased to believe their doctrines. But the value Augustine set on friendship found expression in his later experiences of community life and in the community rule he passed on to the world.

Augustine included a further reflection on the theft of the pears in *The Literal Interpretation of Genesis*, which he started writing around the same time as *Confessions*. He believed that, when Adam accepted the stolen fruit from Eve, he knew that he was disobeying God, but he did not want to disappoint his partner. As with Augustine's own escapade with the pears, the sin arose neither from deceit nor hunger, but from misguided loyalty and careless pride. In seeking to please Eve rather than God, Adam committed sin. So, for Augustine, sin is 'love gone wrong'.

It was not until much later in life that Augustine narrated these youthful experiences. Despite its title, *Confessions* does not contain the kind of revelations we associate with tabloid journalism today. They are in fact confessions of faith, as Augustine reflects on God's unfailing love and goodness towards him from the earliest years of his life. Even so he may have been taking the opportunity to warn others against making his mistakes. There is more than a hint of episcopal sermons in some of the rolling phrases. But Augustine wasn't the first teenager to rebel against a pious upbringing, and he may in fact have been one of the quieter and more temperate members of his gang. Monica was evidently aware of Augustine's sexual adventures, and solemnly warned him not to become promiscuous or to commit adultery.

A friend in deed

The wealthy relative Romanianus now began to play a greater part in Augustine's life. He had already helped with financial sponsorship for Augustine's education. Now he and Augustine became good friends. Augustine describes how Romanianus opened not only his wealth to him, but also his heart. There was a benefit for Romanianus in the relationship, as he enjoyed having Augustine's intellectual brilliance on tap. Romanianus owned a library and was himself an aspiring scholar. He hoped that Augustine would eventually settle in Thagaste and become a tutor for his sons. Augustine may have started to fulfil this role during his year at home in Thagaste, before going to continue his studies in Carthage. He would not be the first young teacher to tutor children during the day and run wild with his friends at night.

'Drunk with wine, bloated from overeating and plunged in rottenness and debauchery.'

SALVIAN, PRIEST OF LÉRINS FROM C. 424, DESCRIBING THE MEN OF CARTHAGE

Carthage

In 370, at the age of 17, Augustine arrived in Carthage, about 170 miles from Thagaste. The journey of several days brought him to the sea, which he had previously imagined only in a beaker of water. Here was the capital of Africa, the 'Alexandria of the West', with a port that drew traders and travellers from all over the world. Many forms of greed, superstition and vice had washed in with the commerce, and for Augustine it would prove a university of life.

There were some distinguished and influential residents in Carthage, not least the proconsuls who lived in the palace overlooking the forum. These were the people who would be interested in Augustine's skill with words and who might favour him with their patronage. One such proconsul was Symmachus, a man of letters and no mean orator himself, who arrived in Carthage at the same time as Augustine. In future years Symmachus would become urban prefect in Rome and recommend Augustine to his cousin, Bishop Ambrose, to be professor of rhetoric in Milan. Symmachus, although he might not have agreed with Augustine, nor even remembered him, would be an important patron at a crucial moment, especially as the young African had to overcome any Roman prejudice against his provincial accent.

Into the frying pan

Carthage led the world in pagan excesses. The mother goddess was Coelestis, the 'Queen of Heaven', who was attended by effeminate eunuchs and celebrated in public portrayals of sex. At the theatres, the lusty escapades of the god Jupiter were enacted in lurid detail, as were the labours of Heracles and the adventures of Aeneas. In the huge amphitheatre, it was not so long since Christians had met their martyrdom in the jaws of wild beasts. There was also a circus, where Augustine could enjoy the excitement of the chariot races; and public baths in the forum, where he would meet with student friends.

In such a place Augustine was under an avalanche of temptation. The word for Carthage (*Carthago*) sounded like the word for frying pan or cauldron (*sartago*), and Augustine appreciated the pun. He was coming to the

'As yet I had never been in love and I longed to love... I was in love with love, and I hated safety and a path free of snares.'

CONFESSIONS 3.1.1

boil himself and dived in with enthusiasm.

Monica's spirit was with Augustine, even in the big city. He continued as a Christian catechumen, receiving preparation for his baptism, even though it might not take place until he was on his deathbed with his sinning days over. He occasionally attended church meetings, if only to look out for pretty girls. The young men and women sat together during vigils, with a good deal of teasing and ribaldry between them, not least in putting rude words to the hymns. Augustine recalled such occasions 30 years later, when he preached in Carthage, on the feast of St Vincent in 405.

Carthage was also a place of wider spiritual quest. Alongside competing forms of Christianity were the occult arts of mediums and magicians, fortune-tellers and astrologers. Augustine, the possibility thinker, was fascinated to think that one's fate could be discerned in the entrails of a sacrifice or the movement of planets. He experimented with these practices for a while, but concluded that they were a form of demon worship. He later believed it was involvement with the occult that prevented some fine thinkers, such as Porphyry, from coming to faith in Christ.

'In those years I had a woman. She was not my partner in what is called lawful marriage. I found her in my state of wandering desire and lack of prudence. Nevertheless, she was the only girl for me, and I was faithful to her.'

CONFESSIONS 4.2.2

'God's gift'?

It may well have been at church that Augustine met the woman who became his partner for 15 years and with whom he had a son. Whether they met in Thagaste or Carthage is not known, but the woman soon became pregnant. They called their child Adeodatus, which means 'given by God'. Augustine never divulged the name of his partner. Adeodatus was almost 15 when he was baptized in the spring of 387, so he must have been born in 372, when Augustine was 18. It is possible that the episode at the baths and the theft of the pears in Thagaste are Augustine's way of saying that he was sexually active and that Adeodatus was conceived in the course of adolescent adventures in his home town.

Augustine had longed to be in love. He had visited the theatre and wallowed in plays that portrayed the pain of love and the parting of lovers. Now the loves and losses of the real world were brought home to him. Towards the end of his first year in Carthage, his father died. It was probably around the same time that Augustine made his commitment to the young woman who would be his partner for so many years.

These experiences sobered Augustine. He was scarcely 20 years old and already he felt his life was careering out of control. He had indulged his sexual appetites, but with regrets. With better guidance, he would have preferred to have made a marriage.

As Monica was now a widow she moved to Carthage. She refused to eat with her son because of his

Why didn't Augustine marry his partner?

Augustine and his partner lived together for 15 years and their much-loved son made them a family. Perhaps Augustine doesn't declare the woman's name because to do so would open old wounds, or embarrass her if she was later living in Thagaste. He was unable to marry his mistress because of the difference in their social standing. She may have been poor, or from a peasant or racially different background. Whatever the reason, the culture of the day was against them. While it was quite usual for someone of Augustine's status to take a lover for a while, in the long term he was expected to make a marriage that would improve his position in society and further his career.

Augustine realized the injustice of this situation. In *On the Good of Marriage*, he will commend the faithfulness of a woman who is wronged when her man moves on to make a society marriage. When Augustine's partner was finally sent away from him, she vowed never to go with another man.

'If only someone could have imposed restraint on my disorder. They would have transformed to good purpose the fleeting experiences of beauty in these lowest of things, and fixed limits to indulgence in their charms. Then the stormy waves of my youth would have finally broken on the shore of marriage.'

CONFESSIONS 2.1.3

'Let him be where he is, only pray the Lord for him... It cannot be that the son of these tears should perish.'

CONFESSIONS 3.12.21

'My love was returned and in secret I attained the joy that enchains. I was glad to be in bondage, tied with troublesome chains, with the result that I was flogged with the red-hot iron rods of jealousy, suspicion, fear, anger and contention.'

CONFESSIONS 3.1.1

Manichaean beliefs, but she continued to pray for him. When she poured out her heart to a bishop, he counselled her to be patient, assuring her that 'the child of so many tears' could not be lost.

Augustine recalls in *Confessions* how much his emotions were in turmoil at this time; that he had 'polluted the spring water of fellowship with the filth of concupiscence'. Looking back, he saw a pure love for God polluted by his passionate quest for human love. With a partner who was now pregnant or with a young child, he found himself caught up in a maelstrom of lust and love, jealousy and joy. He was both a student – wanting the freedom of the libraries and the nightlife of a university town – and a reluctant young father.

Father and son
There was something wonderful and fascinating about baby Adeodatus. Augustine studied his son's development, intrigued by the sucking and sleeping, smiling and crying, physical exertion and mental frustration. For Augustine, who was always as questioning as he was observant, this was a rich seam of discovery and reflection. He could see that 'original sin', in the form of self-seeking and anger, was inherent in human nature from the earliest days of life.

Augustine described his own infancy in imaginative terms: 'I would endeavour to express the intentions of my heart to persuade people to bow to my will. But I had not the power to express all that I wanted nor could I make my wishes understood by everybody' (*Confessions* 1.8.13).

When Adeodatus was 16, father and son would collaborate on a book called *On the Teacher*. In it, they would explore the complexities of human learning and language, symbols, signs and memory. Augustine claimed that learning was a process of God-enabled discovery, stimulated by need and best nurtured by the encouragement and understanding of others. In education, he preferred to get the best from a student by reward rather than punishment. He always remembered how counterproductive were the beatings he received in the cause of learning Greek. In Augustine's opinion, learning was best undertaken in an atmosphere of love, which is a reflection of God's dealings with all his creatures.

'Top of the class'

Augustine was a successful student, showing a special talent for public speaking and making lasting friendships. It was true that he continued to yield to peer group pressure and mixed with a wild bunch he called 'wreckers', but only because he was afraid not to belong. They were the sort of students Augustine would find impossible when he himself became a teacher.

'I was already top of the class in the rhetors' school and was pleased with myself for my success and was inflated with conceit.'

CONFESSIONS 3.3.6

CHAPTER 3

From Manichee to Christian

I n 373, when Augustine had been in Carthage about two years, he read *Hortensius*, by the greatest of Roman orators, Cicero (106–43 BC). This book is now lost, although enough fragments have survived to give an idea of its contents. It was written in dialogue form and expounded the importance of finding and loving wisdom.

For Augustine, *Hortensius* was a revelation. It opened his mind to 'philosophy', which in those days meant a coherent body of teachings that offered a 'world view' of principles and values to live by. For Cicero, 'philosophy' was not a matter of abstruse theorizing, but a highly principled and aesthetically pleasing way of life; almost, in fact, a religion. For the first time, Augustine found himself listening to truth, rather than the mere sound of words. A new stage of his spiritual quest had begun.

Cicero's path to 'wisdom' led through a rigorous programme of self-discipline and self-improvement. The wise man was someone who trained his head to rule his heart and physical passions in order to live a humble and objective life. Cicero taught that by controlling earthly desires and developing reason and knowledge, a person could embark on the way back to heaven. The idea of bringing one's passions under strict control appealed to Augustine, and awakened in him an urgent desire to know God. Like the prodigal son in Jesus' parable, he was coming to himself amid the brothels and circuses of Carthage and realizing how much he was missing the safe haven of Christian faith; but the journey home would take several years.

'The book changed my feelings. It altered my prayers, Lord, to be towards you yourself. It gave me different values and priorities.'

CONFESSIONS 3.4.7

Cicero's book set Augustine searching for his spiritual roots, a coherent philosophy of life, and a better way of writing. Cicero had abandoned elaborate and stylized rhetoric in favour of plain argument and discussion. His books read as a conversation between people seeking the truth – or between a teacher and his circle of pupils. Plato had also favoured this method, which he learned from his own teacher, Socrates. As Augustine enjoyed thinking through issues in the company of others, the idea of writing in the form of conversation or debate suited him well. It bore fruit in a rich harvest of books, letters, sermons and prayers.

'I longed for the immortality of wisdom, with an incredible ardour in my heart. I began to rise up to return to you.'

CONFESSIONS 3.4.7

A bust of Marcus Tullius Cicero (106–43 BC), the greatest Roman orator of his day. Cicero wrote on politics and rhetoric, as well as verse and many letters. He was murdered by political opponents.

*'Augustine
was... sensual
and at the same
time spiritual;
attracted by the
things of this
world and yet
devoted to the
life of
intelligence;
yielding in
friendship on the
one hand and
yet firm to shake
it off on the
other. [He was]
compounded of
excess and
restraint,
imagination and
reason,
mysticism and
dialect. There is
no simple
formula that will
explain him.'*

JOHN O'MEARA, *THE
YOUNG AUGUSTINE*

By the time Augustine read *Hortensius*, Cicero had been dead for more than 400 years. In the meantime, 'wisdom' had become an object of religious passion, expressed in a spiritual quest for a pure way of life. Augustine immediately identified 'wisdom' with the Christian God of his upbringing and devoted himself to seek this God by reading the Bible. In the Old Testament, 'wisdom' is the personification of the godly way of life; a theme that the apostle Paul finds fulfilled in Jesus Christ, 'who became for us wisdom from God' (1 Corinthians 1:30).

Although Augustine turned to the Bible with a fresh appetite, he was sharply disillusioned by its style and content. His copy was the rough translation in Old Latin, which had been made for Africans in the second century by uneducated Greek missionaries. Augustine was offended by the crudeness of its style, which compared badly with the eloquence and dignity of Cicero. He also found no virtue in the faults and failings of the people of the Old Testament and was perplexed by the differing genealogies of Jesus in the Gospels of Matthew and Luke.

Meanwhile, Augustine's circle of friends in Carthage was a great delight to him. The heady combination of love and learning, friendship and the quest for faith, was a foretaste of the Christian communities Augustine would seek to establish in the future. It was at this time that some of the people he found so intelligent and attractive drew him into a radical, exciting and otherworldly form of Christianity, known as Manichaeism.

The Manichees

Augustine was not the only person having difficulty with the Bible. While some of the African bishops had developed Christianity in a legalistic way, with a strict moral code and cramping ritual, some other Christians had broken away from the Catholic Church to live in the true freedom and grace of the gospel. These 'new' Christians argued that they didn't need the Old Testament at all. Instead, they claimed to enjoy a direct and vibrant relationship with the living Christ, who imparted to them his wisdom and power. In Carthage, these neo-Christians formed a gifted, persuasive and fashionable group, which appeared to live out the clear thinking and radical Christianity. They were called 'Manichees'.

The Manichees were named after their founder, Mani (c. 216–76), a self-styled 'Apostle of Jesus Christ'. Mani had received his inspired revelation in Mesopotamia, where he was persecuted and executed by the Persian government in AD 276. His message claimed to be a unique disclosure of the nature of God, humanity and the universe. In effect, it was a Persian adaptation of Christianity, which added in Zoroastrianism, speculative philosophy and superstition. By the time Augustine became a Manichee 'hearer', the founder had been dead for nearly a century. But Mani's mission had been to found the one, true, universal Church.

Manichaeism was taken up with great enthusiasm. It spread throughout the Roman empire and, in later centuries, to the Far East and China, moving from one language to another and adapting to a variety of cultures.

Mani's missionaries arrived in Carthage in AD 297, calling themselves 'The Elect', and living a life of stark self-denial. They spoke of mysteries and secrets, practised strict fasting and abstained from sex. Their holy books were exquisitely inscribed and illuminated volumes of parchment, detailing the secrets and rituals by which fallen human beings could escape from 'darkness' to 'light'.

Those who were attracted to the message of the Manichees (if not to their lifestyle) were called 'hearers'. The movement allowed two levels of membership, whereby someone could make a full commitment or simply join as a seeker or sympathizer. These latter were the 'hearers'.

Augustine was drawn to the Manichees. He was intrigued by their explanation of the existence of evil –

that it was due to the invasion of 'the kingdom of light' by 'the kingdom of darkness'. The 'good' or 'light' that is in every human being and in all the world is being ruthlessly invaded by an entirely separate force of 'evil' or 'darkness'. This way of thinking of good and evil as equal and opposing forces perpetually in tension and at war is called 'dualism'.

The self-styled prophet Mani, whose exotic mix of Christian Gnosticism and Persian mysticism drew many followers in India and the Far East. Fresco from Khotscho, India.

For the Manichees, 'conversion' took place when a person heard Mani's *Letter of Foundation*. It roused him or her to the terrible plight of being held captive by the forces of darkness. Mani urged his hearers to realize the potential of their divine spark – the little glimmer of God that is within every human being. New believers embarked on a course of study and self-denial that would enable them to escape from the powers of evil and avoid all further wrongdoing and other sources of guilt.

The Manichees had an austere vegetarian diet. Melons and cucumbers, which are light and watery, were thought to be especially rich in 'Soul'. They didn't drink wine, even at communion, because it had been fermented and might lead to loss of self-control. They abstained from sex because they believed everything below the waist was the work of the devil. For Mani, sex was to do with the dark, and the dark was the essence of evil. The aim of all this effort was to enable the tiny spark of goodness that is in every individual to escape and be united with the one Soul.

Augustine joined the Manichees. With his wayward

youth behind him, he was an ideal candidate for dedicated study and self-discipline. He was admitted as a 'hearer', which meant that he was allowed to keep his partner and excused the most demanding austerities and rituals. He soon became an ardent evangelist for the cause; confident, eloquent and quick-witted. He could dismiss the arguments of half-hearted and compromised Christians because he had been one himself. Now he was able to feel superior – morally upright and intellectually secure.

Augustine liked the idea of esoteric knowledge and secret paths to salvation; these had already drawn him to dabble in fortune-telling and horoscopes. Manichaeism also appealed to him intellectually as an explanation of the way the world is: split between good and evil. According to Mani, all that is 'good' has emanated from a perfect, pure and innocent god. Unfortunately this 'father of light' is too holy and remote to engage in conflict with 'evil'. This 'good' god was not the same as the God of the Old Testament, who Mani rejected as terrible, violent and immoral. Mani erased all references to the Old Testament from the Christian scriptures. The goal of his religion was not to save the world but to escape from it. In his view all worldly involvement should be avoided for fear of contamination by evil. Jesus, he believed, had been saved by his death, which was passive and unresisting in the face of evil.

Augustine was a Manichee for nine years. He enjoyed the fellowship and sense of purpose, but soon developed doubts about the truth of their beliefs. Manichaeism looked impressive, but it was founded on superstition and myth. It didn't ring true and it didn't work. While it was tempting for Augustine to think that when he sinned it was not his 'pure' self but an evil entity within him, he had to admit that it *was* his real self who was sinning. He questioned the Manichaean insistence that goodness must be passive, and that 'good' was helpless under the onslaught of 'evil'. He couldn't accept that a good God was pathetic and powerless.

Cracks had appeared in the foundation of Augustine's Manichaean beliefs, and the entire edifice would eventually crumble and fall. But the ruin would clear the ground for a much more beautiful and satisfying structure to be built: his Christianity. Augustine's second conversion would be far greater and more lasting than the first.

Return to Thagaste (374–76)

When Augustine had completed his studies in Carthage, he returned to Thagaste and became a teacher. Monica was so opposed to his Manichee views that she would not allow him in the house. We glimpse a stubborn streak in both of them, as Augustine responded by going to live with Romanianus – the patron who had helped his parents to pay for his education.

Romanianus was some years older than Augustine, but the two struck up a lasting friendship. Augustine persuaded Romanianus to become a Manichee, but their life was singularly free of self-denial. They enjoyed eating and drinking, hunting and gambling. Romanianus administered his estate well and was generous with his wealth in supporting the local games and spectaculars. While Romanianus supported Augustine materially, Augustine did much to enrich Romanianus's mind and soul. Augustine began to think of starting a community of philosophers and Romanianus agreed to put up the money for it.

One of Augustine's old school friends became gravely ill. Augustine had persuaded this friend also to become a Manichee, but on his deathbed he was baptized as a Christian. When, to everyone's surprise, he recovered, he was able to tell Augustine of the extraordinary blessing he had received through baptism, even though he was unconscious at the time. When the friend became ill again and died, Augustine found himself overwhelmed by passionate anger and grief.

As Augustine describes his feelings, he echoes the Bible story of Cain and Abel. Cain was furious when his

'I had become to myself a vast problem, and I questioned my soul, "Why are you sad, and why are you very distressed?" But my soul did not know what reply to give.'

CONFESSIONS 4.4.9

What did the Manichees believe?

The Manichees understood the created world as a place of conflict between light and darkness. According to Mani, light and darkness are two equal and opposite principles of good and evil. They are eternally in conflict with one another, and neither is ever able to win. Darkness has pulverized light into a myriad tiny fragments, which are scattered throughout the world as the 'divine spark' of life in all living things: humans, other animals and plants. But through Mani's teaching, these particles of divine light could be released and make their way back to reunion with the source of all Good.

According to Mani, the great spiritual teachers, such as Jesus and the Buddha (and Mani himself), had been sent to help human beings free their divine spark and escape to the realm of pure light. By so doing, they could achieve union with God. This God was not the same as the 'god' of the Old Testament, who had made the world and declared it to be 'very good'. Mani taught that 'matter' (the material world of creation) was actually very bad, forming an evil prison from which humans must seek to escape. He wouldn't allow any references to the Old Testament in his version of the Bible because, for him, Jesus was not the fulfilment of Old Testament promises, but a crucified symbol of humanity.

In effect, Manichaeism was a late form of Gnosticism (*gnosis* meaning secret 'knowledge'). The strictest form of Manichaeism involved self-denial, fasting and celibacy – which enabled people to become members of 'the elect'. But it was also possible to join at a lesser level of commitment, as a 'hearer'. People like Augustine, who were already in sexual partnerships, were allowed to continue as they were, but encouraged to avoid having children. They must do nothing to increase the amount of 'matter' (and therefore 'darkness') in the world.

The first murder.
Cain killing his
brother, Abel,
as told in the
Bible story
(Genesis 4:1–17).

brother Abel's offering was accepted by God while his own was not (Genesis 4:2–16). Cain's jealous anger led him to murder his brother, defy God, and become alienated from society. Writing later in *City of God*, Augustine identifies such anger as a great sin. Cain refused to let go of his anger and wandered far from home, eventually founding the world's first city. For Augustine, rage and pride are at the heart of the Earthly City, which is the opposite and enemy of the City of God. Augustine similarly found himself confused and disorientated by waves of passionate emotion, as he first tried desperately to manipulate the faith of his friend

and then had to mourn his death. Like Cain, Augustine fled – back to Carthage.

Carthage again (376–83)

In Carthage, Augustine became a teacher of rhetoric. Romanianus may have helped Augustine secure this position, which he was to hold for nine years. It was the first step on a career ladder that, for many Africans, had led to heights of fame and fortune in the Roman empire.

Roman education focused strongly on skill with words and effective argument, with close attention to grammar and the rules of rhetoric. Once developed, these skills were used for both political persuasion and personal flattery – and Augustine excelled in both, as his letters show. In today's terms, he was a master of 'spin'.

Augustine enjoyed his intellectual prestige in Carthage. He was proud of his ability to teach himself from the most difficult books. He read Aristotle's *Categories* in a Latin translation and the 'natural philosophers' such as Cicero on the overlapping studies of astrology and astronomy. He could not help but compare the scientific views of the universe with the superstitions and myths of the Manichees. He also read the works of Varro and Seneca, and had long been familiar with the works of Apuleius, the celebrated author from his school town, Madauros.

Augustine persuaded many of his friends and students to convert to Manichaeism, but he was drawing them into a sect about which he himself had doubts. He later described these conversions as 'self-defeating victories'. He knew now that the Manichees were wrong in their understanding of astronomy and began to probe their teaching on religious matters as well. When Faustus of Milevis, the leading Manichee teacher in Africa, visited Carthage, Augustine was able to meet him. Faustus was a charming personality and a compelling orator, but he was entirely unable to answer Augustine's questions. When he readily admitted his ignorance, the two men became friends.

From this point Augustine's enthusiasm for Manichaeism began to fade. He ceased to practise astrology or make sacrifices to placate demons. And it was about this time that he was impressed to hear a simple Christian called Helpidius argue the case against Manichaeism in a convincing way.

Augustine competed successfully in several speech contests, through which he attracted the attention and friendship of influential people. The Roman proconsul, Helvius Vindicianus, crowned Augustine with a garland as victor in a poetry competition, and their brief encounter

Opposite page: 'Pleasant but ignorant' was Augustine's verdict on Faustus, a famed Manichee teacher. The two are seen here engaged in close argument. French illustration on vellum (twelfth century).

Augustine's memory of Faustus

I waited with intense yearning for the coming of Faustus... When he came, I found him gracious and pleasant with words. He said the things [the Manichees] usually say, but put it much more agreeably. But what could the most presentable waiter do for my thirst by offering precious cups?

When I put forward some problems that troubled me, I quickly discovered him to be ignorant of the liberal arts other than grammar and literature, and his knowledge was of a conventional kind.

[Manichee] books are full of immensely lengthy fables about the heaven and stars and sun and moon. I wanted Faustus to tell me, after comparing the mathematical calculations which I had read in other books, whether the story contained in the Manichee books was correct, or at least whether it had an equal chance of being so. I now did not think him clever enough to explain the matter... He knew himself to be uninformed in these matters and was not ashamed to confess it.

This was an additional ground for my pleasure. For the controlled modesty of a mind that admits limitations is more beautiful than the things I was anxious to know about.

CONFESSIONS 5.6.11, 12

led on to a warm and useful friendship. It was Vindicianus who advised Augustine to abandon the astrology of the Manichees, and through Vindicianus that he was introduced to Flaccianus, a student who became proconsul

of Africa in 393. He also met Symmachus (prefect of Rome 384–85), who would help him secure a post as rhetor in Milan and himself had been proconsul at Carthage.

About 380, when Augustine was 26, he wrote his first book entitled *On the Beautiful and the Fitting*. The work has been lost, but Augustine summarizes it in *Confessions* and outlines the basic idea in one of his letters. He argued that the soul within a human being is a spark of the divine nature, so everyone has the potential to progress towards a supreme good. This was the Manichee belief that humans could, by using their reason, win their way to perfection.

Augustine dedicated his first book to Hierius, a famous orator of the day who lived in Rome. He had never met the great man, but hoped the tribute might attract his attention and patronage. The sap of his ambition was rising!

'That orator was of the type which I so love that I wanted to be like him.'

CONFESSIONS 4.14.23

Friends

Despite his doubts about their doctrine, Augustine had continued to enjoy the fellowship of the Manichees. The routine of study, discussion and worship appealed to him, as did the communal reciting of prayers, listening to the reading of the holy books, and sharing the discipline of abstaining from food and sex. Looking back on these years, Augustine praised the integrity and goodness of friends such as Alypius and Nebridius. Alypius was a relative of Romanianus from Thagaste who trained as a lawyer but gave up his career to follow Augustine. He eventually became a bishop in his native Thagaste. Nebridius was a highly intelligent and serious-minded young man, who also became one of Augustine's long-term companions. Augustine mentions other friends, including Honoratus and Fortunatus. Most of them followed him into Manichaeism and then into Christianity, but Fortunatus remained a Manichee and would one day take part in a famous public debate with Augustine at Hippo.

In his teens and as a student, Augustine had been influenced by peer pressure, but now he attracted loyalty as a leader. Friendship stirred in him strong and conflicting passions, which he describes as 'less an appetite of the senses than a hunger of the heart'. Always and increasingly, Augustine's heart-hunger fixed itself on God. It was only in God that his consuming restlessness could hope for peace.

Although Augustine was fortunate in friendship and a gifted communicator, he failed to establish his authority as a teacher. His pupils were reluctant to learn and his classes were constantly disrupted by bad behaviour. He had become disillusioned with

Alypius and Nebridius

Alypius and Nebridius were two of Augustine's greatest friends.

Alypius and Augustine had known each other from childhood. In adulthood, Alypius became an administrative lawyer: a man of action and resolve, with a calmness and firmness of purpose that was the very opposite of Augustine – his 'other self'. Alypius enjoyed the bloodshed of the gladiatorial shows and, when finally converted to Christ, walked barefoot on frozen soil through Italy. He travelled to Italy ahead of Augustine.

Nebridius was a gentler, less ambitious person than Augustine, with wealth and freedom enough to accompany his friend on their spiritual and intellectual pilgrimage. He came from a pagan family in Carthage, which is where he and Augustine became friends. In later life, Augustine remembered Nebridius for his diligence in dealing with difficult problems and his indignation when the discussion was shallow or the disputants took short cuts to their conclusions.

*'For a long time
the Academics
were at the helm
of my ship.'*

ON THE HAPPY LIFE

'Constantine
overcame his
enemies by divine
inspiration.'
Frieze depicting
the emperor
Constantine's
departure from
Milan after
defeating
Maxentius at the
Milvian Bridge in
AD 315. Arch of
Constantine,
Rome.

Manichaeism, without being able to see any other way ahead. In the end he decided to leave Carthage and sail for Rome, having heard that the students there were better behaved.

Augustine seems to have left Carthage in a hurry. Certainly he didn't tell Romanianus, although he was tutor to his old friend's children; and he didn't tell Monica. He may even have lied to his mother, which indicates that he was seeking to escape her prayerfully determined pleas for his conversion. However it was, at the age of 29 Augustine sailed from Carthage with his partner and their son, together with close friends Alypius and Nebridius. Their destination was Rome.

As Augustine sailed for Rome in 383 he was at sea in more senses than one. Thanks to his education in the liberal arts he had seen through Manichaeism. He was attracted to the thoughtful approach and ascetic lifestyle of the Manichees, but realized that at heart they were deeply misguided. His interview with the Manichaean bishop Faustus of Milevis had confirmed his suspicion that their understanding of the universe owed more to astrology than astronomy; and if they were wrong on that, what confidence could he have that they would be right on anything else?

How to be wise?

Thanks to his reading of Cicero, Augustine was fired with
the ideal of living a true and consistent life, guided by
wisdom. But where could wisdom be found? His search of
the Christian scriptures turned up violence and immorality
in the Old Testament and inconsistency in the New.
Thanks to his mother's prayers and unfailing support,
Augustine was a Christian by upbringing; but he was
not so by conviction. There was no bridge between the
philosophers and Christ.

So Augustine took his stand on the high ground of
scepticism. Cicero had founded an academy where the
prevailing view was sceptical – that is, that one had to live
life with dignity and integrity despite the absence of God
or any assurance that life had meaning. This was a similar
view to that of the Greek Stoic philosophers: to live
without hope of reward, salvation or afterlife, and yet
show a detached consideration, respect and selfless
goodwill to all creatures.

Milan and Ambrose

On arriving in Italy, Augustine and his party went first to
Rome. Suddenly, instead of being well known for his talent
and potential as he was in Carthage, Augustine was just

Ambrose, the
celebrated bishop
of Milan,
surrounded
by saints and
serenaded by
angels in a
painting by Alvise
Vivarini and
Marco Basaiti,
Venice (1503).

one more hopeful wordsmith in the vastness of the Roman empire. But when a competition for a post as public teacher of rhetoric in Milan was announced, he entered and won. It was 384.

Milan was the main seat of government for the western empire. Here Augustine encountered the formidable figure of Ambrose, who was 14 years his senior and had been bishop of Milan for 11 years. Ambrose was a tough political operator. In 386 he held his ground against the demands of the imperial court that was resident in his city, infiltrated by Arian heretics and supported by Gothic troops. He built a basilica and triumphantly secured its status by interring the relics of two martyrs. But it was as a preacher that Augustine was drawn to Ambrose, first for the eloquence of his sermons and then for their content. This man's mind held the bridge between Cicero and Christ. Ambrose gave Augustine the means of understanding the Old Testament and showed him that it was faith that led to wisdom and not wisdom that led to faith. The key stage of enlightenment was to accept the truth of the scriptures whose authority was guaranteed by the Church. It was the scriptures and the Church together that led to Christ.

Ambrose was a highly gifted and influential man who dominated not just the religious but also the political scene in Milan. He had a powerful mind and Augustine was immediately impressed by the quality of his preaching – and this from someone who was an outstanding communicator himself. In Ambrose, Augustine found someone who could communicate at his own intellectual level, confirming his rejection of the Manichees and opening the way for his return to the Christian faith and the Catholic Church of his upbringing.

Neoplatonism

Ambrose and others in his circle were strongly influenced by the writing of Plotinus, the father of Neoplatonism. The Neoplatonists, as they were called,

'I came to Milan, to Ambrose the bishop, known throughout the world as the best of men, devout in your worship.'

CONFESSIONS 5.13.23

Ambrose, bishop of Milan

Ambrose (c. 339–97) was born into a noble Roman family
and received a classical education. He rose to the position
of a provincial governor in northern Italy, living at Milan.
When Auxentius, the Arian bishop of Milan, died in c. 373,
Ambrose succeeded him by popular demand. He reluctantly
agreed to accept the post, although he was not yet
baptized or ordained. He then began his study of theology!

Ambrose was a gifted preacher and his fame soon
spread. He upheld the orthodox faith against Arianism
and was conspicuously successful in maintaining the
independence of the Church against the civil power. He
was a close adviser of the emperor Theodosius and was
one of the first church leaders to use his episcopal office
to influence and coerce civil rulers. Augustine had great
respect for Ambrose's stature, eloquence and intellect.
Ambrose's synthesis of Christian and Platonic thought, and
his ability to interpret the Old Testament allegorically, were
significant factors in Augustine's conversion to the Christian
faith as practised by the Catholic Church.

Ambrose encouraged monasticism in the west. He
wrote on asceticism, ethics and the sacraments. He
composed many Latin hymns that have survived into
modern times, and his letters are of lasting historical
significance. Augustine availed himself of Ambrose's
knowledge of Greek to introduce eastern theology to the
west. He also commissioned a hagiography (a devotional
biography in praise of a holy life) of Ambrose from the
bishop's former secretary, Paulinus of Milan.

Opposite page:
**'A gifted
preacher.'
Augustine and
Monica sit
listening to a
sermon from
Bishop Ambrose
in a painting by
Ambrogio il
Bergognone
(1455–1535).
Turin, Italy.**

*'I was not stable
in the enjoyment
of my God. I was
caught up to you
by your beauty
and quickly torn
away from you
by my weight.'*

CONFESSIONS 7.17.23

drew together the insights of Christian thinkers from
east as well as west to synthesize the revelation of the
Christian faith with the insights of the classical Greek
philosophers. Like Plato, Plotinus started from the
assumption that reality is intimately connected with the
process of human thought. He described the structure of
things along the lines of Plato's analysis of identity and

Plotinus

Plotinus (205–70) was a pagan Greek philosopher who had
been influenced by Christian ideas. He was born in Egypt and
studied in Alexandria. After investigating the philosophy of
Persia and India (and almost losing his life on a military
expedition to Mesopotamia), he arrived in Rome in 244. There
he founded a school of philosophy, which became a hub of
intellectual activity in the pagan and Christian world.

Plotinus lived an ascetic life with very little food or
sleep. He ate only vegetables and never took a
bath. His own body and person seem to have
been of little interest to him, as though he
were living as independently of them as
possible. He never celebrated his birthday. He
was a progressive, wise and popular teacher
who (unusually for those days) taught male
and female students together. They sought out
his advice on the problems in their lives, much
as one might consult a spiritual director.

Plotinus's achievement was to rediscover the
authentic teachings of Plato, and indeed many felt that he
was a reincarnation of the greatest of Greek philosophers. In
old age he even tried to found a model republic in Campania,
based on Plato's prescription for an ideal state.

**The head of
Plotinus, here
portrayed on a
European coin.**

difference. According to Plato, if we say two things, x and y, are similar, we mean both that they are alike and different. Although they are alike, we can still make a distinction between them; but even as we point up the differences, we are identifying their similarity. From this, Plotinus follows Plato in establishing that there is a unity and permanence that underlies and undergirds multiplicity in differences we experience and perceive in this world. Even as we talk of change, we imply a permanence that is unchanging.

This concept of changelessness is an aspect of a world of Being that we can grasp only by the use of our mind. We cannot access Being through the usual channels of our senses because they are always engaged with the continuous activity of Becoming that occupies us in the physical world. Those things about the material world that we consider to have special qualities of beauty, goodness or truth, derive their qualities from Absolutes or Forms. But Forms are those constant and unchanging realities that underlie and enable Universal Being. They are invisible to us and undetectable by our physical senses, yet can be identified through pure mathematical abstraction. They are ultimately real and universally true.

Starting from Plato's perception, Plotinus expounded the divine realm as a great chain or continuum of 'being'. At the summit of this hierarchy of being is the One, or God, that Plotinus called the Absolute, or the Unknowable. All existence emanates from the One in a series of layers or levels – each layer of being taking its existence from the level immediately above it. But because the cause is always greater than the effect, each subsequent emanation is lesser or lower than the level that causes it. The further something is from the source of ultimate Being, the more likely it is to be inferior or imperfect; but this imperfection can be overcome by returning to the source of goodness and truth, the One. Because the One is unchanging, it never loses its virtue

'By the Platonic books I was admonished to return into myself. With you as my guide I entered into my innermost citadel, and was given power to do so because you had become my helper. I entered and with my soul's eye, such as it was, saw above that same eye of my soul the immutable light higher than my mind – not the light of every day... but a different thing, utterly different from all our kinds of light... It was superior because it made me.'

CONFESSIONS 7.10.16

'How unhappy I was, and how conscious you made me of my misery, on that day when I was preparing to deliver a panegyric on the emperor! In the course of it I would tell numerous lies and for my mendacity would win the good opinion of people who knew it to be untrue.'

CONFESSIONS 6.6.9

and perfection; it is never diminished despite its timeless giving of existence to all that is.

Plotinus, however, rethought many of Plato's concepts and, through his own teaching, established the school of philosophy known as Neoplatonism. Plotinus's theory of existence allowed the Perfect Cause, or God, to be the source and sustainer of a material universe. It offered an explanation of how the One could be both transcendent and involved in the process of existence. It presented a possibility that imperfect or inferior beings might be restored by returning to their absolute and pure source. It accounted for the existence of evil as a loss of perfection as things exist further from absolute goodness.

Plotinus believed that human beings could retrace the path of emanation to attain reunion with the One and claimed to have experienced this four times during his own life. Christians also speak of similarly being reunited with God; of humanity sharing divinity.

Plotinus discerned a divine trio at the summit and source of all existence: the One, Mind and Soul. The One alone is supremely good. Everything else may demonstrate and experience goodness but will necessarily be less than perfectly good. Mind is less perfect in that it manifests pride and self-seeking. Soul is further still from perfection and has the power to produce matter. Matter is the opposite of Form – evil, formless, nonbeing. Such evil is of a cosmic, non-moral character. It is better spoken of as imperfection rather than evil. But Plotinus offered two further explanations of evil that address the question of where moral evil in human experience originates. The first was that it originated as a consequence of misused freedom, arising from the potential for weakness in human beings, resulting from their inferior place in the ladder of Being. The second was that it originated from the weakness of the human soul, which tended to lead it to become preoccupied with material things. Because of their imperfection, arising from lessened Being, this human preoccupation with material things becomes the root of moral evil in the soul of a person, causing its fall.

The Neoplatonists enabled Augustine to think through the problems of whether 'matter' is good or bad and where evil comes from. He read several books by Neoplatonist writers including *The Enneads* and came to see that he had the light of truth within himself – a light that was intelligible, offering insight, reason, understanding and choice.

Augustine came to see evil as the absence, loss or

'I anxiously reflected how long a time had elapsed since the nineteenth year of my life when I began to burn with a zeal for wisdom, planning that when I found it I would abandon all the empty hopes and lying follies of hollow ambition. And here I was already thirty, and still mucking about in the same mire in a state of indecision.'

CONFESSIONS 6.11.18

Porphyry

Plotinus died in 270, but his many long and complex discourses were edited, shaped and published by his disciple Porphyry as *The Enneads*. Porphyry was a Greek from Tyre, less intuitive than Plotinus, but a well-trained academic philosopher. He was the author of a popular work, *The Return (to Heaven) of the Soul,* and has been described as the first systematic theologian in history. Although attracted to Christianity at one time, he wrote a famous – even notorious – work, *Against the Christians*.

While Plotinus was a supremely detached individual, Porphyry was more restless and engaged with the passions and possibilities of human existence. He declined to believe that the human quest for God was purely rational, delved into alternative spiritual paths such as Indian yogi and the occult and – at the age of 70 – married a widow with eight children. Augustine called Porphyry *doctissimus* – 'the most notable pagan philosopher'.

Plotinus and Porphyry laid the foundation and provided the structure for the philosophical quest of the next three centuries. As Neoplatonism was then taken up by Augustine, it was to have a profound effect on the development of Christian theology in the west.

'What will this wretched man do? "Who will deliver him from this body of death" except your grace through Jesus Christ our Lord (Romans 7:24)... In him the "prince of this world" (John 14:30) found nothing worthy of death and killed him, and the "decree which was against us was cancelled" (Colossians 2:14). None of this is in the Platonist books.'

CONFESSIONS 7.21.27

Augustine's conversion in a garden, depicted by Fra Angelico (c. 1387–1455). Musée d'Art Thomas Henry, Cherbourg, France.

corruption of the good. Evil was the product of fallen humanity. But how could one be delivered from this evil and move towards this good? He was restless and disillusioned with his speech-writing at the imperial court, where his prime task was to flatter the people in

power. He despised himself for prostituting his gift with words.

It was at this point that Augustine was ready for the teaching of Paul, that Christ is not just a teacher but the 'saviour' or 'redeemer' of the human race. Paul taught

*'In the agony of
indecision I
made many
physical gestures
of the kind men
make when they
want to achieve
something and
lack the
strength… Yet
I was not doing
what with an
incomparably
greater longing
I yearned to do,
and could have
done the
moment I so
resolved. For as
soon as I had the
will, I would
have had a
wholehearted
will. At this
point the power
to act is identical
with the will.'*

CONFESSIONS 8.8.20

Opposite page:
A sixteenth-
century Greek
ikon of Antony of
Egypt, one of the
greatest of all the
Desert Fathers.

that Christ is the perfect One who entered and embraced the fallen, material world and mediated to it the transfiguring grace of God. The Manichees saw Christ as a teacher but Christianity and Paul recognized Christ as the Redeemer. But Augustine was used to the idea of working hard for salvation, by self-denial and sacrifice. Should he renounce all earthly joys and ambitions? He readily gave up his prospects of a brilliant career in provincial government and with much more difficulty resolved to live a celibate life. It was the beginning of August 386.

'Pick up and read'

Monica joined Augustine in Milan, bringing with her his brother and two cousins. There was nothing to hold them in Thagaste and they were free to share the benefits of Augustine's good fortune. If his career in government was to progress, he now needed to advance his position in society by marrying someone of wealth

Antony of Egypt

Antony of Egypt (c. 251–356) was one of the first Christian hermits. In c. 269 he gave away his possessions and devoted himself to the life of asceticism, retiring into the desert c. 285. He is said to have fought with demons disguised as wild beasts. His discipline and holiness attracted huge numbers of disciples and in c. 305 Antony returned from the desert to organize them into a community of hermits who lived under a common rule.

Antony returned to the desert in c. 310 but was later influential in supporting the Nicene party against the Arians. The *Life of Antony of Egypt*, probably written by Athanasius, was highly regarded throughout both the east and the west for its teaching on Antony's asceticism and as a masterpiece of hagiography.

and social status. Monica negotiated such a marriage to a young girl and with great agony of heart Augustine sent his partner of many years and the mother of his son back to Africa. She vowed she would never take another man and may have entered a religious community. Augustine found to his dismay that he could not live without a sexual relationship and took another mistress until his fiancée should be ready for marriage.

Augustine was torn. Like Paul before him, he found he couldn't do the things he wanted to do and instead did the things he didn't want to do. His philosophy called him to a life of abstinence and self-control, but his physical passions mastered and overwhelmed him. He tried to reconcile this very human battle by praying that God would give him continence – but not yet.

Ambrose had shown Augustine how to understand the Old Testament in terms of allegory. He now turned to the Bible with a fresh appetite, no longer put off by the poor Latin translation.

One day Augustine received a visit from an African Christian, Ponticianus, who was surprised to find the professor of rhetoric reading the letters of Paul. Ponticianus told Augustine and his friend Alypius the story of Antony of Egypt, who had lived a life of supreme holiness as a hermit in the desert. He was surprised that they had never heard of the Desert Fathers or the monastic communities that had become so popular among those seeking a closer devotion to God.

Hearing about Antony filled Augustine with a great sense of shame. How far he was from this kind of devotion to God! On the contrary, despite his high ideals he was a slave to self-indulgence and lust. Going into a garden with Alypius, he was in an agony of inner conflict. He felt his will 'pitting myself against myself'. Why couldn't he simply desire and do what was best?

In the garden, as he wept beneath a fig tree, Augustine heard the voice of a child somewhere nearby. It was chanting the rhyme of a game: '*Tolle lege, tolle lege*'

'Not in revelling and drunkenness, not in debauchery and licentiousness, not in quarrelling and jealousy. Instead, put on the Lord Jesus Christ, and make no provision for the flesh, to satisfy its desires.'

ROMANS 13:13–14

('Pick up and read, pick up and read'). Running into the house, Augustine picked up the copy of Paul's letters that he had been reading earlier, and opened it at random. His eye fell on some words from the letter to the Romans, chapter 13, which were to change his life.

He told Alypius what had happened. His friend took the book and read on, finding the words 'Accept anyone who is weak in faith' and applied them to himself. Together they found Monica, to tell her that her prayers had been answered – and to share in her joy.

'I neither wished nor needed to read further. At once, with the last words of this sentence, it was as if a light of relief from all anxiety flooded into my heart. All the shadows of doubt were dispelled.'

CONFESSIONS 8.12.29

CHAPTER 4

The Road to Ordination

Augustine had been converted to Christianity, but his struggle had been as much over lifestyle as belief. As he described it later, he was yielding finally and completely to a way of discipline and self-denial, which he had always believed was the authentic path of discipleship, but never been able to embrace.

Cassiciacum

Augustine's first action was to gather Monica and some like-minded people around him to form a kind of monastic community. A friend Verecundus, who was a grammarian in Milan, lent him a villa about 19 miles north-east of the city, at Cassiciacum (probably modern Cassago-Brianza) near Lake Como on the foothills of the Alps. They lived there for nearly a year. The villa was large and surrounded by fields, with baths where they could meet together when the weather was bad. In the event, the weather was often beautiful, though cold.

There were ten of them altogether – a mixture of relatives (Monica, Adeodatus and Navigius), cousins (Lartidianus and Rusticus), friends (Alypius and Nebridius), and pupils (Licentius and Trygetius). If Augustine was still doing work for the court, there may have been some additional staff of servants and secretaries; but part of the exercise was to live in community and to share the daily chores. This was 'leisure' – the freedom and space to think and learn. In the context of this shared life, Augustine wanted to teach, discuss and reflect. He wanted to digest and integrate the

Revelation and reason

In the *Cassiciacum Dialogues*, Augustine explores his new-found conviction of a harmony between faith and reason. He had repudiated and rejected Manichaeism and turned to the scepticism of Cicero and the New Academy. But scepticism, while being intellectually satisfying, did nothing to slake his spiritual thirst. Now Plotinus and the Neoplatonists had opened up for him a philosophy that embraced the life of the spirit, giving him confidence in the philosophical quest for wisdom. And Ambrose had given him confidence in another exhilarating area: the revelation of Christ in the scriptures.

Augustine celebrates the marriage of reason and revelation, although the union was never consummated by Plotinus or his disciple and successor Porphyry. While Augustine was glad to check the revelation of Christ against the assured conclusions of reason, there was not much traffic coming in the opposite direction. The incarnation of Christ that is central to Christianity was passed over in silence by Plotinus and scorned by Porphyry. Some scholars feel that the *Cassiciacum Dialogues* show that Augustine is still not thoroughly converted, and that the dialogue form allows him to explore the problems and doubts with which he continued to struggle.

Early Christian, third-century coarse stone mosaic of Christ. Museo Ostiense, Ostia, Italy.

In the days before diaries and autobiographies, the *Cassiciacum Dialogues* are Augustine's own aide-memoire of his spiritual and philosophical quest: a period of emotional, intellectual and religious upheaval. He will revisit these memories in *Confessions*, which, although in the form of a prayer, will be the first autobiography ever written.

insights of Neoplatonism and Christianity, and to draw together the intellectual and religious strands of his life as he, Alypius and Adeodatus prepared themselves for baptism.

Augustine was recreating something of the fellowship he had enjoyed with his Manichee friends in Carthage, when they had spent time studying the Bible, discussing Cicero and Virgil, and praying the Psalms. This experiment in Christian community was an ideal he would pursue for

Lake Como in Italy as it is today. It was near these peaceful waters that Augustine and his friends made their retreat at Cassiciacum.

'In nothing shall I depart from the authority of Christ, and reason will find truth with the Platonists, and this will not oppose our sacred mysteries.'

AGAINST THE
SCEPTICS 3.41–43

the rest of his life. He might be ascetic, but he was never solitary.

The community at Cassiciacum was celibate. Verecundus was unable to join them because he was married. Augustine's partner had been sent back to Carthage, although their son Adeodatus stayed with his father. When Augustine had heard of the example of Antony, he had been shamed to think that someone who wasn't even a philosopher had attained such heights of

'Myself reflecting with myself for some time on various things, and persistently for many days quizzing myself over what I should seek, what avoid, I suddenly addressed myself.'

THE SOLILOQUIES 1.1

*'Alone with
each other, we
talked very
intimately... We
asked what
quality of life the
eternal life of the
saints will
have... While we
talked and
panted after it,
we touched it in
some small
degree by a total
concentration of
the heart.'*

CONFESSIONS
9.10.23, 24

spiritual purity. In those days it was the philosophers who
were expected to achieve control of mind over matter.
'Self-control' meant abstinence from sexual activity in
particular, as it was regarded as the prime behaviour of
the 'lower' nature. Even the wise and objective Marcus
Aurelius (121–80) had dismissed sexual intercourse
as 'the release of slime' (*Meditations* 2.15), while the
emperor Julian the Apostate (332–63) likened lust to
'a crazed and ruthless despot' (*Ammianus* 5.4.2).

Because the idea of progress from evil to good and
from darkness to light had more than a dash of the old
Manichaeism in it, some have concluded that Augustine
remained a Manichee all his life. But with Christianity,
self-denial was no longer an end in itself, but the means
of focusing his devotion on God. In place of the old
frustration and self-loathing, Augustine found release
into freedom and peace. He was no longer a Manichee,
fighting the entrapping evils of the material world, but
saw all the good things of creation as God-given; only to
be handled with care, lest they be loved or desired more
than the Giver. Asceticism and dedication belonged
together as two sides of the perfect freedom: a single-
minded devotion to God.

The insights of Neoplatonism would continue to
exercise a profound influence on Augustine's thinking
as a Christian theologian and bishop, particularly in his
understanding of the nature of evil and his exposition of
the Trinity.

At Cassiciacum, Augustine began to write with vigour
and freedom. Until now (he was 32) he had written only
On the Beautiful and the Fitting. In the course of a few
months at the villa, he produced four books in dialogue
form. They were presented as the outcome of the daily
discussions and are known as the *Cassiciacum Dialogues*:
Against the Sceptics, *On the Happy Life* and *On Order*, and
The Soliloquies.

Augustine evidently felt that he had discovered a
guiding principle that could be expounded in many

Opposite page:
**Bishop Ambrose
baptizes
Augustine in the
baptistry of Milan
cathedral on
Easter Eve.
Painting by Bicci
di Lorenzo
(1373–1452),
Museo Bandini,
Milan.**

Monica with
Christ rising from
the grave and a
sainted bishop,
perhaps
Augustine,
standing nearby.
From a series of
paintings by
Francesco Botticini
(1446–97)
depicting
Monica's
foundation of the
Order of
Augustinian Nuns,
in the Church of
Santo Spirito,
Florence, Italy.

directions: education, the arts, philosophy and religion. In this he seems to have been following Manlius Theodorus, from whom he had borrowed books in Milan. Theodorus had retired from his position as consul to devote himself to philosophical writing. Augustine now dedicated *On the Happy Life* to him. Although Theodorus was a Christian when Augustine had first met him in the Neoplatonist circle at Milan, he later reverted to paganism.

As he dedicated one book to Theodorus and another to Romanianus, Augustine began to narrate and comment on his own life story. In effect, he stumbled on a way of talking to himself that became autobiography, resulting first in *The Soliloquies* and eventually in the *Confessions*.

But Augustine was not merely talking to himself; he was testing, challenging and probing his own attitudes towards the issues that preoccupied him. He called the exchanges *Soliloquies* to distinguish them from monologues. Important, too, were the many incidents and conversations that took place within the little community – and the

connections Augustine was able to make between everyday happenings, the workings of philosophy and the life of the soul.

Baptism at Milan

Augustine returned to Milan in the spring of 387, ready for his preparation for baptism. Along with the other candidates, he went unwashed through the Lenten period and wore a hair shirt as a sign of penitence. Instruction in the Christian mysteries was given by Bishop Ambrose, the Creed and the Lord's Prayer were committed to memory, and the candidates were baptized by Ambrose himself – after an all-night vigil – at sunrise on Easter Day. It was 25 April.

After his baptism, Augustine remained in Milan for a while, resuming his philosophical friendship with the Neoplatonists, Simplicianus and Theodorus. His immediate interest was to prove that the soul is immortal and he wrote about this in *On the Immortality of the Soul*. He then conceived a project to produce a series of books that would lead people from the liberal disciplines to the higher perceptions of the spirit. To this end, he made a start on the first two volumes: *On Music* and *On Grammar*.

'We were baptized, and disquiet about our past life vanished from us.'

CONFESSIONS 9.6.14

Ostia and the vision with Monica

Augustine was now committed to living in a community. In the summer after his baptism he journeyed south, with Monica and a few friends, by way of Rome to the seaport of Ostia. Their intention was to return to Africa and form a community there for prayer, study and the service of God. At Ostia their voyage was delayed by the outbreak of war between the emperors of east and west and the usurper Maximus. In a house overlooking a garden, Augustine and Monica were talking of the joys of eternal life when they experienced a shared vision. Augustine describes how they were caught up beyond all earthly concerns, to touch wisdom 'in some small degree' in a moment of 'total concentration of the heart'.

Monica confided in Augustine that she was now content to die, having seen her prayers answered that her son should become a Christian. In the event she contracted a fever and died nine days later. She was buried at Ostia but her remains were later interred beside the high altar at Augustine's church in Rome. A part of her epitaph was discovered at Ostia in 1945.

Tribute to Monica

Augustine paid affectionate tribute to his mother. From his formative years he had been profoundly aware of her Christian faith and lifestyle in contrast to his father's paganism. It was she who had created a loving home, its harmonious atmosphere hallowed by prayer. Augustine recognized that his independence of mind and life had caused her much heartache, but she had never ceased to desire and pray the best for him.

'There is no nature, and absolutely no substance, which does not possess in itself and manifest, first that it is, then that it is this thing or that thing, and thirdly that it remains as much as possible in the very thing that it is.'

LETTERS 11

Many questions have been asked of Monica's obsession with Augustine – after all, she had other children to consider as well. Her prayers and tears seem to indicate a controlling nature that could barely let her favourite son out of her sight. But Augustine had by no means been tied to his mother's apron strings. From the age of 12 when he went to school in Madauros until he left to take up his studies in Carthage, he was only at home in Thagaste for a year – and much of that was spent in burgeoning independence as he stayed with Romanianus and took up with the young woman who became his partner.

In Book 9 of *Confessions*, which deals with the time at Ostia, Augustine includes a brief memoir of his mother. It may be that his appreciation of her had only flowered during the months at Cassiciacum, as Neoplatonism challenged Augustine to be more open to the education and opinions of women. Although Monica lacked a formal education, she was observant, intelligent and witty; and she shared her son's ability to make connections between the everyday world and abstract concepts.

In their vision at Ostia, Monica and Augustine, mother and son, were able to transcend such barriers of intellectual or emotional difference that were between them, and 'enter the joy of their God'. Plotinus claimed to have had 'out of the body' experiences, but attributed them to his ascetic lifestyle and exalted thoughts. Augustine could see that, in Monica's case, there was no such determination to 'ascend'

For Romanianus

Augustine wrote *On True Religion* before his ordination in 391. In it, he seeks to persuade his old friend Romanianus away from Manichaeism to a contemplative form of Christianity.

In the prologue, Augustine writes warmly of Platonism and remarks how compatible it is with Christianity. Augustine believed that if Plato had lived in the Christian era he would have embraced Christianity. Augustine then presents a range of solutions to the problem of evil other than that proposed by the Manichees, and deals at length with 'the ascent of the mind to God' – a theme that dominates so much of his early thinking. He examines the relationship of faith and reason, and the role that carnal desire, pride and curiosity play in human spirituality and development. He concludes with an epilogue in which he exhorts the reader to adore the triune God – the 'Holy Trinity' of Father, Son and Spirit.

On True Religion is a short and masterly work. Augustine explores the concept that vice is a false imitation of the divine. For him, both philosophy and religion are a quest for happiness: the happiness of truth that is desired, discovered and lived. Vice might offer self-knowledge through immoral behaviour, but this would lead to guilt and regret rather than freedom and joy. Only in true religion is found true happiness, because it is centred on the worship of the one true God.

to ecstatic experience. Their vision was entirely 'of grace' –
a gift. And it was shared.

A year in Rome

As the port of Ostia was under blockade, Augustine and his
group were unable to sail for Carthage as they had planned.
Instead, they returned to Rome. When Augustine had first
arrived there from Africa, he was a fledgling orator moving
freely in the influential circles of his Manichaean friends.
Now he was a Christian, intent on expounding answers
rather than speculating questions. His ambition was to
write books.

The political atmosphere in Rome was volatile. One
pope had died and his successor had been driven out of
town. Augustine's mentor Ambrose was lending his weight
to a new pope, Siricius, to curb the aggressive persecution
of Christians by the usurper Maximus. Much as Augustine
admired Ambrose, he did not involve himself in the
bishop's power-broking.

Augustine stayed in Rome until after the death
of Maximus in summer 388. During this time he was
entirely focused on the monastic life and the task of
writing books. He continued to use a dialogue approach –
this time in conversation and debate with his friend,
Evodius, who had left his post with the imperial secret
police in Milan to travel with Augustine to Africa.
Augustine completed a dialogue entitled *How to Measure
the Soul* and began work on the two-volume *On Free
Choice* – which would remain unfinished for nearly
a decade. He also wrote prepared short answers to
questions raised by friends that, along with others added
at Thagaste and Hippo, would eventually appear as *On
Eighty-Three Different Questions*.

Community at Thagaste

By the autumn of 388 the blockade was lifted and
Augustine and his group sailed for Carthage before winter
closed the sea routes. Arriving in Africa, Augustine and

Alypius stayed with a former official named Innocentius, who was miraculously healed of a painful fistula. It was while visiting Innocentius that Augustine met a local deacon, Aurelius, who was to become bishop of Carthage and be his senior colleague for 35 years.

Augustine also visited his young friend Nebridius, who was in poor health, but living in a grand manner with his mother near Carthage. The two corresponded 'of Christ, of Plato, of Plotinus' and Augustine declared the letters of his friend 'the apple of my eye'. Nebridius must have thought of joining the community at Thagaste – but his poor health and the cost of sacrificing his comforts made such a move impossible. Their enforced separation stimulated a fascinating and valuable correspondence, which has survived. Nebridius put so many questions to his learned friend that Augustine complained that the answers were beyond the intelligence and time of anyone to provide. Even so, they explored the nature of knowledge and the characteristics of imagination, memory and enlightenment. They also continued a discussion about the incarnation and the nature of the Trinity that had begun at Cassiciacum.

Arriving in Thagaste, Augustine and his friends set up a lay monastery in the old family home. Most of the property was sold and the money given to the poor. They settled into the daily routine of a contemplative life, which had 'leisure' in the true sense of the word – time and space to seek God and become like God.

The reading and discussion within the community inspired Augustine to further intellectual endeavour. With Adeodatus he wrote a dialogue work called *On the Teacher*, in which they investigated the nature of words and the causes of learning. Augustine praised Adeodatus for his brilliant answers, but sadly the young man died the following year. He was 17. If his mother had come from Thagaste and returned there, it is possible that she would have been able to be with him in the last weeks of his life.

'We associated with us the boy Adeodatus, my natural son… I contributed nothing to that boy other than sin. His intelligence left me awestruck.'

CONFESSIONS 9.6.14

Anti-Manichaen writing

Augustine deeply regretted the part he had played in
persuading friends and colleagues to join the Manichees.
In 388, the year after his baptism, he began to write and
publish arguments against Manichee beliefs – a running
battle that would last some 15 years. He knew at first
hand their elaborate myths and superstitions and was able
to expose their scientific ignorance of the nature of the
universe. He also had evidence (perhaps from Constantius
himself) of their hypocrisy.

At Rome he had begun to set the record straight with
the first of many written works against the Manichees,
entitled *On the Catholic and Manichee Way of Life*, which
included a graphic description of a so-called 'self-denying'
Manichee who enjoyed a superb standard of living. It was
started in Rome and finished in Thagaste.

Because the Manichees claimed to be reasonable,
Augustine set out to argue reasonably with them. He
defended the Old Testament scriptures against the
Manichee criticism that its patriarchs and God were
primitive, coarse and immoral. For the first time, he
engaged in comparing the Old Testament with the New,
to demonstrate the coherence and integrity of the Bible's
message. He also argued that the asceticism that was
found among Christians in Egypt and Italy was superior
to that of the Manichees. In *Against the Sceptics* (written
in autumn 386) Augustine wrote that true happiness
is not to be found in virtue alone but in loving the
transcendent goodness of God. Asceticism must give
way to a higher authority, which is the teaching of the
scriptures.

Augustine upheld the Catholic and Orthodox Church
as the custodian of these scriptures and therefore the
institution that guaranteed and commended the values
that held family, society and state together. He compared
the inconsistency of Manichaean morality with the
stability and depth of the Church, which was centred on
and formed by love. The books proved popular and were

*'By his
conversations
and books he
taught both
those who were
present and
those who were
absent.'*

POSSIDIUS, C. 370–440,
LIFE OF AUGUSTINE

circulating widely in Africa by the following year.

Augustine also addressed the problem of evil. He argued that evil is in fact a *lack* of something that a thing or being ought to have. The supreme good is God, who alone lacks nothing and will never decrease in essence. Augustine attacked the Manichee elect by exposing the hypocrisy and decadence of their much-vaunted asceticism. In condemning matter as evil, they denied the goodness of creation – but they didn't object to partaking of 'sacred' food when it was offered!

The first five commentaries on Genesis were written in the context of the community at Thagaste in 389: *On Genesis Against the Manichees*. Augustine was attempting an exposition of the accounts of creation in Genesis. It was a theme to which he would return many times. He wanted to write a Catholic commentary on the book of Genesis, which would also serve to oppose the Manichees; but in fact he found it very difficult to interpret Genesis literally and had to resort to explaining it as allegory. He rebutted the Manichaean objections to Genesis, but not without some selective reading of the text himself. His view begins to emerge that the world is not a spiritual obstacle to be despised, but a creation to be used for attaining the enjoyment of God. Around this time Augustine also wrote his first ecclesiastical pamphlet. Returning to his home town and realizing his identity as an African Christian, he wanted to defend the faith against the myths of the Manichees. As an African to Africans in Africa, he wrote in a simple and accessible style.

'Let us put off all empty duties and put on useful ones. As for exemption from care: I do not think that any can be hoped for in this world.'

LETTERS 18

A public role

The community at Thagaste was rather different from that at Cassiciacum. At Cassiciacum, Augustine had wanted privacy and the company of friends. At Thagaste his reputation and therefore his life was more public. Augustine and Alypius were 'servants of God' – dedicated, well-educated Christian laymen who mixed with the leaders and patrons of the Church. In addition, Augustine

was now a distinguished intellectual in his own right
and his advice was sought not only by friends and
acquaintances, but increasingly by correspondents. The
'servants of God' were a resource for the Church, objects
of interest to pagans, and role models of perfection to
their weaker brethren. In the next generation, it was
Pelagius who would cash in on the Roman preoccupation
with the 'perfect' life.

Getting involved

When writing to Nebridius, Augustine had spoken of the
ideal of 'growing god-like' in retirement – in other words,
envisaging a secluded life of prayer, reflection and self-
improvement. But with a person like Augustine such a
state of spiritual equilibrium couldn't and didn't last. His
sense of identification with, and responsibility for, his
fellow Africans was strong. As we shall see, the African

The site of the
Roman forum in
Hippo Regius
(modern Annaba
in Algeria). The
town was
captured by
Vandals in 430
but rebuilt by
Arabs in the
seventh century.
The fine basilica
dedicated to
Augustine is seen
in the distance.

Christians were struggling for survival against the
Donatist schismatics as well as the Manichees.
Augustine the man of action must interrupt the
contemplative retirement of Augustine the man of
leisure. Nor could he be the uninvolved observer of
affairs that he was as a foreigner in Milan or Rome.
In Thagaste he was a local.

In an age when suitable individuals were seized and
compelled into ordination by the acclamation of local
congregations, Augustine already knew to beware of
ecclesiastical ambush, as he remembered what had
happened to Ambrose in Milan. Augustine began to avoid
visiting places that were without a priest, or where the
bishopric was vacant, in case he also was called. But in his
own mind he was abandoning the systematic exposition of
the liberal arts on which he had embarked. He completed
the sixth chapter of the text *On Music* at Thagaste, but the
rest of the series was given up. Instead, he began to write
material that would defend and commend the Christian
faith in this African setting.

*'By no means
did I seek to be
what I am... It
pleased the Lord
to say "Rise up".'*

SERMONS 355:1, 2

In the course of five years, Augustine's life had
undergone great changes. By 390, when he was 36, he had
said farewell to his partner and suffered the deaths of his
mother and son. His friend Nebridius also died. But in
that time he had become a Christian, started to write and
establish his reputation, and founded a monastery where
he was regarded as a spiritual father. He emerged from
this spiritual and emotional upheaval with a strong resolve
to use the rest of his life to good effect.

Call to ordination

Augustine was strongly committed to the monastic life,
where individuals submitted themselves to each other
out of Christian charity, united by their love of God and
their commitment to the authority of a superior. In 391,
he visited Hippo Regius, partly to visit a Christian friend
who was a member of the imperial secret police; but also
with the idea of establishing another monastery. While

there, he was suddenly called by the local church to be its priest.

The elderly bishop of Hippo, Valerius, was a Greek-speaker who was unable to understand the Punic

Hippo Regius

Hippo Regius (modern Annaba in Algeria) was a major and prosperous port in Augustine's time, situated on the coast about 34 miles from Thagaste. It had been a Roman city for 200 years, and was the principal city of 'Proconsular Numidia', where today Tunisia borders eastern Algeria. It was governed by a deputy or 'legate' of the Roman proconsul in Carthage.

Hippo provided a natural harbour for the grain fleet that transported wheat and other cereal crops across to Ostia to feed the population of Rome. The river Seybouse afforded natural landing places and access to the agricultural plains of the interior where the crops were cultivated. Archaeologists have unearthed a huge Roman forum, a large theatre, an imposing temple, and impressive public baths. The remains of villas fronting the sea, with vestiges of beautiful mosaics and statues, indicate a wealthy and cultured society; albeit one that had peaked and was losing its vigour.

As time and tide silted up the ruins of Hippo, Arab traders assumed it was the baths that had once been Augustine's cathedral. In fact his bishop's 'quarter' – church and chapel, house, monastery and garden – lay between the main hill and the harbour, well away from the pagan and political centre of the town: the temple and the forum. While Roman institutions were underfunded and becoming dilapidated, there was plenty of private wealth on show in the features and furnishings of individual houses. The sea gave access to a wider world and enabled the flow of visitors and letters; but Augustine was not himself a traveller in the usual sense.

It was the emperor Nero who had decided to take grain from Africa rather than Egypt. To this end he commandeered large estates to secure the necessary food supplies for an empire that was always hungry; but in so doing he created an underclass of marginalized and disaffected peasants. These landless seasonal workers were recruited by religious groups, especially the Donatists, to provide an intimidating rabble of supporters in the doctrinal disputes of the day.

language of his flock. He was also ineffective against the Manichaean presence in Hippo, which was headed by the popular 'bishop' Fortunatus (a friend of Augustine's in Carthage days), and the Donatist schismatics, led by their bishop Faustinus. The Donatists were so influential that they were able to forbid the bakers to provide bread for the Catholic community. Valerius needed a gifted assistant with immediate effect – and there, walking into his church, was Augustine! Like Elijah calling Elisha, he gave the younger man little room for refusal. Augustine was acclaimed by the congregation as God's choice and hauled before the bishop for ordination there and then.

Augustine would recall how he had wept at his ordination – not out of joy or frustration, but because he had previously thought so little of such people; their faithfulness, desires and needs. Possidius adds that he was even then aware of his inevitable advancement to the episcopacy, with its huge pastoral, intellectual and physical workload. To be called was a privilege, but Augustine only agreed to be ordained if he was allowed to build a monastery near the church.

Augustine teaching, as imagined by the illustrator Maxwell Armfield in an edition of *Confessions* (1909).

Augustine would live at Hippo – in a house with a garden, near the cathedral–church – for the next 40 years. In a letter to Valerius after his ordination as priest, he requested study leave – 'a little time' – so that he could increase his understanding of scripture in preparation for his ministry. He also needed to adjust his mindset from contending with fellow intellectuals to communicating the faith to simple people.

Augustine's output of writing is astonishing. He produced some 5 million words in books, pamphlets and sermons. This was achieved, no doubt, because he was accompanied by secretaries – a practice that would have started in his days as a professor of rhetoric in Milan and certainly continued when he was a bishop preaching around his diocese.

Books were copied by hand and circulated by the author and his readers. Entire manuscripts were parcelled up and sent with messengers to fellow scholars and interested groups. One hindrance to the progress of a publication was any lack of copyists; another was a shortage of suitable *carta* – the antecedent of paper.

Letter to Honoratus

The Manichees had a strong presence in Hippo and among them was Honoratus, another friend of Augustine's from Carthage days. Augustine wrote Honoratus a long letter, which became a small book entitled *On the Advantage of Believing*. He urges Honoratus not to dismiss the Bible without at least understanding it better. They would not have dismissed the writers they admired in their youth, Virgil and Terence, in such a way. He distinguishes between a faith that is produced for the ulterior motive of attaining happiness and a faith that is based on trust in the one true God attested by the authority of the Church. For this he quotes Isaiah: 'Unless you believe you will not understand' (Isaiah 7:9). For Augustine, faith is a step on the way to knowledge.

Knowing that Honoratus is a sophisticated thinker, Augustine delicately tries to argue for the primacy of faith over reason. He distinguishes faith from gullibility and identifies it more with 'trust' in a wise person, of whom Christ is the supreme example. At his simplest,

Augustine will say 'If you cannot understand, believe in order to understand; faith precedes, understanding follows'; but Honoratus may have found that short cut unconvincing.

In later works, Augustine changed his mind about *On the Advantage of Believing*. He came to believe that humans cannot in fact attain ultimate happiness – that is, the permanent vision of God – in this life. Rather, he agreed with the apostle Paul that in this earthly and temporal existence humans are unable to see God clearly ('for now we see in a mirror, dimly' – 1 Corinthians 13:12).

Martin of Tours divides his cloak to share it with a beggar. By this simple gesture he became the most popular saint in France. *Master of the Fallen Angels*, fourteenth century. The Louvre, Paris.

Paulinus (c. 353–431)

Paulinus was born into a noble and wealthy Aquitaine family and educated at Bordeaux. He trained as a magistrate and served as a governor of Campania. On retirement, he married Theresia, who was herself from a noble family, and settled on his family estates in Aquitaine. He became a convert to Christianity and was baptized sometime before 390. The couple went to live in northern Spain.

When their son died, Paulinus and his wife took a vow of continence and began to distribute their possessions to the poor. On Christmas Day c. 393 Paulinus was ordained priest in Barcelona. In the following year he and Theresia left Spain to lead a monastic life at Nola in Campania. Paulinus became bishop there sometime between 403 and 413.

Paulinus had personal dealings with many of his famous contemporaries, including Martin of Tours, Ambrose, Jerome and Augustine. He left a large collection of letters, some of which have survived to shed valuable light on events at the turn of the fifth century. He was also one of the foremost Christian Latin poets of the early Church.

He also criticizes himself for saying that humans can only be wise or foolish. In the course of his arguments with Pelagius (which we will cover in Chapter 6), he realized that children are born with original sin but are hardly guilty of personal sin; they are neither wise nor foolish.

In 391 Augustine followed up his letter to Honoratus with a more general letter to all the Manichaean friends of his youth. He called it *On the Two Souls* – by which he meant the two 'natures' of body and soul that the Manichees believe are at war within each individual. Augustine argues the impossibility of this psychic duality by denying that evil has any positive reality. For him, each human has a single soul that enjoys free will – and it is from free will, not 'matter', that evil arises. Augustine considers that evil could actually be attracted to good, although it is an absolute opposite and has nothing in common with it. He explains how he was taken in by the Manichees and flattered by his own success at persuading others to join them. He had been ignorant of some of their implausible beliefs about the nature of evil and their path to freedom and light. He now believed that sin was an act of will.

In 395 Augustine sent a copy of his book *On Free Will* to Paulinus of Nola. Paulinus and Augustine never met in person but they corresponded for a quarter of a century. Because Augustine was restricted by his episcopal duties in Africa, he sent his books to Paulinus for distribution in Italy.

The debate with Fortunatus

In August 392 Augustine took part in a two-day public debate at Hippo. His opponent was Fortunatus, whom he had known in Carthage and who was now the Manichee 'priest' of Hippo.

Augustine famously opened the debate with the words: 'I now regard as error what I formerly regarded as truth. I desire to hear from you who are present whether my supposition is correct.' He then offered a devastating

'Sin is the will to keep or obtain what justice (in the sense of a morally reproachable act) forbids and from which one can freely abstain.'

RECONSIDERATIONS
1.15.4

critique of Manichee beliefs. Fortunatus's defence was that the Manichee beliefs might be misguided, but their moral behaviour was exemplary. Augustine steered the debate towards doctrine rather than morals, and found the audience on his side. Fortunatus proved a clumsy and evasive disputant, quoting scriptures out of context and sidestepping Augustine's questions by posing others. The audience adjourned in uproar to continue the discussion in small groups.

On the second day, Fortunatus outlined the Manichee belief on the origin of evil, insisting that it had nothing to do with God. Augustine agreed, but then explained his belief that moral evil is a necessary consequence of humankind being given free will. Fortunatus replied that if God had given humans a free will that enabled them to sin, then in some measure he was a party to evil and colluded with it. The debate reached stalemate, as neither could present a logical account of the origin of evil. Augustine then found a way forward by comparing the Christian God with the God of the Manichees. While the Christian God takes a loving risk in creating human beings with free will, the Manichee God crushes the spiritual potential of humankind by imprisoning the soul in evil 'matter'. Fortunatus was unable to answer this point, conceded defeat and left the town.

Augustine had taken centre stage in a form of public debate that was as entertaining as it was instructive. He had a talent for this kind of encounter and would soon be called on to defend the faith against other opponents as well.

Leader and Bishop

As priest of Hippo, Augustine had the pastoral care of a congregation and community that had its fair share of superstition, bad habits and laziness. He was obliged to admit the limits to human perfection, not least in himself, which was a far cry from the idealism of his Neoplatonic conversion.

Just to persuade Africans not to swear oaths (for example) required the breaking of a habit as strong as the use of language itself. Indeed, it was compulsive force of habit (*consuetude*) that Augustine now identified as the seat of the struggle with sin: the fact that the memory had hoarded a store of wicked experience that continued to excite, seduce and entrap the soul in a state of spiritual death. Augustine began to realize that perfection in this life was only ever going to take the form of fleeting glimpses.

The dilemma led Augustine to a deeper engagement with the letters of Paul and especially the letter to the Romans, on which he was lecturing and hoped to write a commentary. Until now, he had assumed that Paul advocated the idea that the Christian individual is 'a new creature': 'If anyone is in Christ, there is a new creation: everything old has passed away; see, everything has become new!' (2 Corinthians 5:17).

Now, however, he discovered that the 'new' life was not so straightforward. Paul himself wrote to his readers in Rome: 'I am of the flesh, sold into slavery under sin. I do not understand my own actions. For I do not do what I want, but I do the very thing I hate' (Romans 7:14, 15).

Augustine discovered Paul teaching a life of conflict between 'flesh' and 'spirit' that would only be resolved in death and a share in the ultimate victory of Christ. His

*'Sometimes you
cause me to
enter into an
extraordinary
depth of feeling
marked by a
strange
sweetness. If it
were brought to
perfection in me,
it would be an
experience quite
beyond anything
in this life. But I
fall back into my
usual ways
under my
miserable
burdens. I am
reabsorbed by
my habitual
practices. I am
held in their grip.
I weep profusely,
but still I am
held. Such is the
strength of the
burden of habit.
Here I have the
power to be, but
do not wish it.
There I wish to
be, but lack the
power. On both
grounds I am in
misery.'*

CONFESSIONS 10.40.65

image of spiritual progress was now no longer an 'ascent' but a long and arduous journey, of travelling rather than having arrived. The realization humbled him in some degree, and sensitized him to the failures of others to some extent.

Augustine refused to despair. As a way forward, he reflected on 'delight' as a true motivator of the human will, alongside the intellect. But 'delight' is not subject to human control: it can appear surprisingly and disappear depressingly. As to those whom God delights in, Augustine had to admit he had lost his former certainties. God does not judge by human goodness, intelligence or education; so in all probability the scholarly idyll at Cassiciacum had not been a taste of heaven after all.

The tombs of the martyrs

There was a widespread custom in the African Church of honouring the departed, and especially the martyrs, by sharing *agape* meals and other celebrations at their tombs. These occasions, which were not restricted to anniversaries, were often the excuse for parties with excessive drunkenness and carousing.

Augustine was anxious to tackle this blasphemous and licentious behaviour and wrote to his acquaintance, the deacon Aurelius who was now bishop of Carthage and primate (most senior bishop) of Africa. The outcome of their correspondence was the calling of a council at Hippo on 8 October 393 – the first such council to be held outside Carthage and an indication of the high regard in which Augustine was already held among his peers. The council prohibited the banquets, but it was still left to Augustine to handle the local celebration of Leontius (the *Laetitia*) at Ascensiontide in 395. By dint of sermons comparing the fruit of the Spirit to the fruits of drunkenness, and the behaviour fitting to Christians compared with that of the Donatists (who could be heard partying in their basilica), he succeeded in carrying the day – but not without contemplating his resignation during the tense hours when defeat loomed.

Augustine becomes bishop of Hippo

Augustine became bishop of Hippo soon after he turned 40, probably in the summer of 395. As bishop, he had the care of the churches in his diocese, as well as the immediate supervision of the monks in his monastery, some of whom were training for ordained ministry and would themselves become priests and bishops. As chief pastor, he was concerned for the poor, orphans and widows in his area, the visitation of the sick, and the protection of his people in the face of oppression by the civil authorities. As a bishop he

Augustine is consecrated as bishop in this painting by Ambrogio il Berognone (1455–1535), Galleria Sabauda, Turin, Italy.

The demise of paganism

On 8 November 392 the emperor Theodosius had banned attendance at pagan temples throughout the empire and sacrifices even within private homes. The decree, which was published in the east, had little immediate effect in Italy. In Africa, Count Gildo also sat lightly to imperial directives until he was deposed in 398. In 395 Theodosius died and was succeeded by his son, Honorius, who was able to impose his religious policy through his regent Stilicho.

On 1 January 399 Flavius Manlius Theodorus took office as consul of the west. He was the Christian dignitary whom Augustine had met in Milan in 386 and to whom he had dedicated *On the Good Life*. On 29 January 399 a new law was promulgated at Ravenna, banning pagan cults. On 19 March, the counts of Africa, Gaudentius and Jovius, acting on the emperor's orders, dismantled temples and destroyed idols. In

Limestone stelae mark the graves of infants who were sacrificed in a flaming pyre to the god Baal-Hammon and his consort Tanit. Sanctuary of Tanit and Baal-Hammon, fifth century BC. Carthage, Tunisia.

Carthage, the Christians, led by their bishop Aurelius, seized the temple of Juno Caelestis, the patron goddess of the town. But although paganism died politically from this point, it could not be so easily erased as an influence in the popular culture.

presided over an ecclesiastical court that heard civil cases. As custodian of the churches, he was responsible for their maintenance and administration – a task he found difficult to delegate to suitable lay people.

Augustine usually preached twice a week, on Saturday and Sunday, but this would increase to every day if he was travelling through an area, or spending some weeks in a centre such as Carthage, or preaching during the Lenten season. As sermons were one of the main means by which Christians were taught, they were akin to a lecture or 'teach-in' and could last for an hour or more. Court cases often required his attention every day – sometimes for whole days at a time. And he involved himself in the councils and controversies of the wider Church, both in Africa and further afield. This meant that he (reluctantly) undertook long journeys and engaged in extensive correspondence with adversaries and colleagues. As always, there were secretaries on hand to take the dictation of his letters or note the words of his sermons.

As an advocate of the orthodox faith and a defender of church unity, he worked ceaselessly to counter the influence of heretical groups such as the Manichees, the Donatists, Pelagians, Arians and pagans. These opponents did not raise their heads conveniently in sequence, to be dispatched one at a time, but presented a combination of challenges and distractions throughout his episcopacy. Paganism, at least in theory, was a spent force; but in reality continued to hold sway in society and in the hearts and behaviour of many people.

Against the Donatists

In the spring of 397, the struggle against the Donatists in Carthage was at its height. After the Manichees, the Donatists presented the second great challenge of Augustine's polemical career.

The Donatists were zealous and passionately committed Christians who broke away from the Catholic

Church in North Africa between 308 and 311. The occasion
of the split was a disagreement over the election of a new
bishop of Carthage, but the causes went back to the years
303 and 304, when the Church was cruelly persecuted by
order of the emperors Diocletian and Maximian. Some
church members had compromised or renounced their
faith in order to survive, while others had held fast and
been imprisoned or killed. The bishop of Carthage,
Mensurius, substituted heretical books for the scriptures
and handed them over instead; but a neighbouring bishop,
Felix of Thibiuca, refused to do any such thing and was
imprisoned and beheaded. So a split emerged in the
Church between 'confessors' and 'traitors', which often
ran along the racial, economic or geographical fault lines
between groups, such as the Carthaginians and
Numidians.

The Donatists (as they were to become known)
identified with the martyrs. They were fiercely critical of
their fellow Christians (Catholics) who had collaborated
with the persecutors by committing *traditio* – that is,
'handing over' copies of the scriptures to be confiscated
or destroyed.

When the time came to elect a bishop, these radically
committed Christians rejected the Catholic candidate,
Caecilian, because one of the bishops who consecrated
him (Felix of Abthugni) was suspected of betraying the
scriptures during the Great Persecution. Instead, they
elected their own bishop, Majorinus. It was Majorinus's
successor, Donatus, whose name was given to the new
movement by the authorities and other opponents;
but the Donatists referred to themselves simply as
Christians.

On becoming emperor, Constantine upheld the status
of Caecilian, but the supporters of Majorinus demanded a
hearing in Rome. This was held at the Lateran in October
313, when Donatus appeared for the first time as the
leader of the schismatics. Although his appeal was
rejected, this was only the first of many such battles. In

317 the imperial government ordered the dissolution of all Donatist communities and the transfer of their basilicas to the Catholics. The Donatists were brutally suppressed and several were martyred, but the predictable effect was that their numbers grew. Constantine was obliged to become more tolerant towards them and by 336 they were able to assemble

'The lusts of the flesh and the pride of life'

On his conversion to Christianity, Augustine had renounced lust, greed and ambition; but he was still troubled by dreams! He blamed this on those past experiences that had furnished 'the vast halls of memory' and over which his subconscious had no control. He was reluctant to enjoy food and treated it as a necessary medicine, except for the occasional feast. Nor was he tempted to overindulge in drink, as he remembered his mother's warning of how she got into the habit of tippling when she was a young girl.

Augustine was a keen observer, and tried to discipline the lustful gaze of his youth into an appreciation of the natural world. For him 'inner light' was all-important and he seems to have been wary of giving full rein to his senses. Scents did not attract him, but he found some music enchanting – especially that which reminded him of the church in Milan. For him, it was the words that were important in acts of worship. Catholics in general had a reputation for rather lacklustre singing – certainly in comparison with the more exuberant Donatists.

As to worldly ambition, Augustine had long since renounced a 'successful' career; but he was now a prominent, even distinguished, person in his own right. He admitted that vanity was the hardest of sins to avoid, to be countered only by grace.

The roots of the Donatist schism

The Donatist schism was rooted among the nomadic farm workers and poor landed peasants of North Africa. Before the arrival of Christianity, they worshipped 'Saturn', a cosmic god to whom they offered animal sacrifices. This in turn had its origins in the older worship of a Punic god Baal-Hammon and his partner Tanit who were worshipped in human sacrifice. There was a tradition of mobility among these people, with passionate feeling, violence and bloodshed in their religion. They could be fanatical to the point of committing ritual suicide.

At root, the Donatists were expressing an African tradition of thought and spirituality. Their members were the older Berber and Punic peoples of the region. Their form of Christianity had posed no problems in the third century, as it was orthodox in local terms. But with the arrival of Roman government, with its imperial structures, wealthy landowners and military might, the local people found themselves marginalized. Those of Donatist persuasion retreated to the remoter, less developed, less affluent areas, and the highlands of Numidia. There they asserted an authentic faith and vigour, which didn't depend on worldly status or wealth. They were the 'original' Christians of North Africa and they cared little for the Roman determination to bring African worship and structures into line with European practice and create a universal Church.

In 250 the Christian Church had been persecuted by order of the emperor Decius. When forced to offer sacrifices to the gods of the empire, Christians had reacted in contrasting ways. While some had killed themselves, others had bought certificates to vouch that they had complied. In the spring of 251, Cyprian the bishop of Carthage had to handle the fallout between Christians – the hard-line 'confessors' and the soft-edged 'lapsed'. After the councils of 251 and 252 Cyprian decided to pardon those who had compromised, but barred them from being ordained as priests. When a further question arose as to whether those who had renounced their faith should be rebaptized, Cyprian believed they should. By contrast, the Church in Rome was content with penitence and the laying on of hands to restore lapsed believers to the fellowship. In September 258, Cyprian himself was martyred in Carthage during the fierce persecution of Valerian.

270 bishops for a conference in Carthage.

Donatus was bishop of Carthage from 313 until about 355. The split, or 'schism', between Catholic and Donatist Christians lasted over a hundred years, until the Vandals invaded North Africa in the early fifth century. The Donatists were a divisive and distracting feature of church life in North Africa throughout Augustine's time as a bishop.

The Donatists had two gifted leaders, first Donatus and then Parmenian. On the Catholic side, Optatus, the

The emperor Trajan (r. AD 98–117) offers sacrifices before war with the Dacians. Column of Trajan, Rome.

bishop of Milevis in Numidia, wrote some spirited criticism of the Donatists, but his six books did not appear until 366 or 367. His writings, together with those of Augustine, are a major source of information on the Donatist church. Some documents of the Donatists themselves also survive, celebrating the martyrs and recording the Donatist councils. One of their own authors was Tyconius, an orator and lay theologian, whose writings impressed Augustine. Tyconius was unusual for a Donatist, because he argued that the Church must necessarily include a mixture of people, both bad and good. With such views, Augustine was surprised that Tyconius remained a Donatist and did not join the more tolerant and inclusive Catholics.

When Constantine became emperor, the Donatist schism meant there were two groups of Christians in North Africa, both claiming to be the official Church. The Donatists accused the Catholics of political intrigue and compromise and established a wide area of influence through their zealous and enterprising evangelism. The hostility between the Catholic and Donatist communities became a long-running feud. In 340, the Circumcellions began to roam the countryside, posing as a holiness movement but in fact stirring up a peasants' revolt, attacking landowners and freeing slaves.

In 347, Constantine's son, the emperor Constans, appointed two commissioners, Paulus and Macarius, to investigate the Donatist schism. Their approach was reasonable, offering help to the Donatist communities, but rejected by Donatus as interference by a persecuting government. At Vegesela (Ksar el-Kelb) in the province of Numidia, Macarius arrested and flogged a delegation of ten bishops. One of the bishops, Marculus, was either executed or committed suicide by a fall from a high rock. He was venerated for this sacrifice and his story added to the many similar 'passions' that strengthened the Donatist claim to be 'the church of the martyrs'.

'Circumcellion' comes from the Latin *circum celliones*, meaning 'those who prowl around homes'. The Circumcellions were violent, superstitious and even debauched, but they saw themselves as 'warriors of Christ', intent on conflict and welcoming martyrdom. Although they sided with the Donatists, they were an embarrassment to the Donatist bishops, who were unable to control them. They brought the Donatists' cause into disrepute, while at the same time defending the Donatist churches against Catholic persecution. According to Optatus of Milevis, the Circumcellions were so far out of control in 343 that the Donatist bishops requested military intervention to suppress them.

Taking on the Donatists

Augustine, through his writings, is one of our main sources of information about the Donatists. He traced their beginnings to the election of the two rival bishops for Carthage, and noted that the Donatists were the party claiming purity by rebaptizing Catholics.

Augustine believed Donatism arose from selfish ambition and lack of understanding and love. It wasn't a split about doctrine so much as the need of a particular group to assert its superior faith. The Donatists, for example, refused to recognize baptisms that had taken place outside their own 'true' church. They insisted that Christians joining them from the Catholic Church should be rebaptized; and they rejected the authority of the Catholic bishops whom they believed were tainted with the compromises of the *traditores*.

The beliefs of the two groups, Donatists and Catholics, were much the same, but the Donatist controversy raised questions about what it actually meant to be the Church. The Church in North Africa was the heir of Cyprian

A Donatist saint,
depicted in a
mosaic found in
Carthage (fourth
or fifth century).

(bishop of Carthage, d. 258), who had insisted on rebaptizing Christians who came into the larger Church from small unorthodox sects. He had taught 'separateness' – that is, that the 'world' and the 'Church' were incompatible: the 'world' was contaminated with sin while the 'Church' was morally pure. For Cyprian, the Church was a holy and separate enclave for Christian saints in the midst of a wicked and demonic world. This meant that the Church's sacraments (baptism and communion), together with its bishops and ministers,

must all be 'pure' – among other things, guarding against foreign influences from 'across the sea' (a favourite Donatist phrase).

Cyprian was a spiritual giant who had been first exiled and then executed for his faith. His influence continued in North Africa for several generations after his death. This gave a strong local identity to the Christians in North Africa, in the face of the empire-building tendencies of Rome and Europe. The native North Africans might be poor and ignorant in the eyes of the world, but they were pure and faithful in the sight of God.

Augustine disagreed with the sectarianism of the Donatists, but never lost his respect for the African tradition and the teaching of Cyprian. He learned from the Donatist theologian Tyconius that the Church must needs contain sinners and therefore be a mixed body of people. This in turn affected the way he thought about the nature of the Church and its sacraments, as well as

A popular song

Augustine realized that he must counter the Donatists at the level of popular sentiment even before he tackled the task of theological debate. Towards the end of 392 or 393, he wrote a popular song, a 'Psalm Against the Donatists'. It had none of the classical form and metre of his Latin education, but was designed to lodge in the mind and on the lips of ordinary, uneducated people. It told them the story of the Donatist split and argued the case for reunion with the Catholics.

A sequence of 20 verses beginning with the letters of the alphabet were followed by a chorus of 'You who delight in peace, now judge what is true.' It closed with 'Mother Church' inviting the Donatists to return to unity with the Catholics. Augustine may have written this song in response to similar efforts by Parmenian, the Donatist bishop of Carthage.

themes such as judgment and the identity of the Church in the world.

Augustine's understanding of Donatism was helped by Optatus of Milevis who had written a history of the controversy. Augustine found a letter of Parmenian against Tyconius, a lay theologian in his diocese. Tyconius had taught that the Church was diffused throughout the entire world and that the sins of one Christian do not contaminate others in the Church. Although this controversy had taken place at the start of the 380s, Augustine used Parmenian's letter as a springboard for his own attack on contemporary Donatists. He wrote his *Against the Letter of Parmenian* in 400.

In the first of three books Augustine criticized what

Augustine's health

In general, Augustine seems to have enjoyed good health. As a boy, he was taken ill with an attack of breathlessness that almost precipitated his baptism in case he was about to die. As an adult he suffered a fever when he first arrived in Rome; and some kind of pulmonary complaint gave him the excuse to resign his professorial chair in Milan. Towards the end of 397, he was unable to walk, sit or stand because of haemorrhoids. But overall he was able to exercise his exceptional capacity for work, both physical and mental.

As he grew older, Augustine complained that he was less able to do all that he wanted to do. Long journeys, in particular, were demanding of his energies, and he avoided travelling in cold weather or high winds. The coastal climate of Hippo sometimes had a penetrating dampness that got into his bones. When he was 75 he excused himself from attending the dedication of a church explaining, 'I could come, were it not winter; I could snap my fingers at the winter, were I young.'

he saw as an inconsistency in Donatist ecclesiology: that Donatists did not rebaptize those returning from schisms in their own church but did rebaptize those coming in from the Catholic Church. In the second book Augustine wrote about the attributes of the Church. He claimed that the Donatists could not be the one true Catholic and Orthodox Church because they had broken communion with the churches outside Africa. He also critiqued the Donatist claim to purity: their priests were as sinful as any other and their people took part in the violence of the Circumcellions.

Augustine argued that the ministers of the sacraments could not contaminate other members. The validity of a sacrament did not depend on the minister but on the action of the Holy Spirit. If a person did not lose the sacrament of baptism or holy orders by sinning or schism, he could continue to administer baptism in schism. The efficacy of the sacrament, however, would be impeded until the recipient returned to the true Church. This is the first explicit distinction of validity and effectiveness in sacramental theology.

'Nothing in you do we hate, nothing detest, nothing denounce, nothing condemn, except human error.'

SERMONS 359.5

In the last book, Augustine connected the unity of the Church with charity and recommended mutual correction. He argued against excommunication and in favour of uprooting the evil from within the individual. This first major work against the Donatists established the fundamental thesis that in the unity of the Catholic Church and in the communion of the sacraments evil does not contaminate the good.

It wasn't until the 390s that support for the Donatists began to wane – beginning in Carthage, where the Catholic bishop Aurelius and the recently ordained Augustine presented them with vigorous opposition. In 405 the Edict of Unity established sanctions against the Donatists, making them liable to punishment as heretics. In 411 a huge convention was organized in Carthage, which tried to limit and even ban their activities.

'The clear
winner of the
Assembly was
Augustine, the
verbal
technician
of his age,
impassioned,
wary,
discriminating
and deadly.'

PAUL MONCEAUX,
*HISTOIRE
LITTERAIRE DE
L'AFRIQUE
CHRÉTIENNE* 4.425

'Assembly' at Carthage

In 410 the tribune Marcellinus was sent by the emperor
Honorius to deal with the rising tide of violence from the
Circumcellions. The Catholics had requested that the
peasant bands should not be allowed to take refuge in
the sanctuaries of Donatist bishops after committing such
crimes.

Marcellinus brought the bishops of both sides
together for a *collatio* or 'Assembly' at Carthage. He dealt
with them very fairly. He restored to the Donatists the
churches that had been taken from them under the
terms of the Edict of Unity. He also guaranteed them safe
passage on their journeys to and from the conference.
In advance of the Assembly, he established an agreement
that the Catholics would surrender their churches and
offices if they were found to be heretical. For their part,
if the outcome was that the Donatists should be reunited
with the Catholics, they would still be allowed to keep
their churches and offices.

The Donatist bishops turned out in considerable
numbers, to make a show of strength. Once there, they
challenged the validity of the consecration of some of
the Catholic bishops, including Augustine whom they
reproached with his distinguished record as a Manichee.
The Catholics were fewer in number and later in arriving,
but in the end the Assembly was between 284 Donatist
bishops and 286 Catholics.

Marcellinus told each side to nominate seven
speakers, seven advisers and four recorders. The Donatists
not only insisted that they should all be present, but
refused to sit down with the Catholics. Marcellinus
patiently accommodated their demands. Because of these
and other procedural wrangles, the atmosphere was very
tense. Augustine advised Catholics to stay away from the
area to avoid being drawn into violence.

When the debate finally began and the history of
the *traditores* was laid out, the Donatists continued to
be obstructive. Augustine argued the case for a 'mixed'

Marcellinus

Marcellinus was a tribune after Augustine's own heart, and Augustine dedicated the first volume of *City of God* to him. Sadly, Marcellinus was himself caught up in a purge after an attempted coup and executed in 413. Augustine tried to save him but, as we have seen before, the bishop of Hippo was no Ambrose of Milan when it came to imposing his will on the civil power. The episode was deeply disillusioning of any hope Augustine may have had that Church and State could work in partnership for good.

Church, citing the parable of the wheat and weeds growing together. The Donatist bishop Emeritus of Caesarea, replied with a bombardment of scriptures to the effect that an evil world was in rebellion against a holy God. Augustine had plenty of ammunition on God's *love* for the world, which he offered in the face of much heckling from the Donatist side. All in all, in the company of some fine speakers, it was Augustine who carried the day.

The Assembly ended on 8 June, and Marcellinus ruled that it was the Donatists who were in breach of the heresy laws. In an edict of 26 June, the Donatists lost their churches, were forbidden to hold meetings, and fined for not attending the Catholic Church. The enforcement of the edict was inevitably patchy, but some Donatist leaders lost their churches, some Circumcellions committed suicide, and there were random and gruesome acts of terrorism. Augustine preached reconciliation, begged for mercy for the terrorists, and shared his basilica at Hippo with a Donatist bishop. Even so, there is little evidence that the stand-off between Catholics and Donatists eased. The schism dragged on through the lifetime of Augustine and the Vandal occupation of North Africa that began in 430. But the Vandals brought a much stiffer challenge to

'If you accuse, accuse from love. If you correct, correct from love. If you spare, spare from love. Let love be rooted deep in you, and only good can grow from it.'

SERMON ON 1 JOHN

the Catholic Church – that of Arianism. By the time North Africa came under Byzantine rule, a hundred years later, the rival communities of Catholic and Donatist Christians had somehow merged. In due course, the term 'Donatist' came to mean any rebellion or dissent against orthodox faith and practice.

Controversy Never Far Away

Although Augustine had routed the Donatists in debate, the heresy continued to blaze throughout the African Church during his lifetime. Further controversies awaited Augustine's attention as he sought to articulate the Christian faith and defend the authority of the Church. From his ordination as a priest in 391 to his death in 430, a vast amount of writing was devoted to this end.

Against Pelagius

Pelagius was born in Britain and learned his theology in Rome. He was a big man, committed to an ascetic life, who believed that human nature was basically good. Augustine read Pelagius's work *Nature* in 415 and was immediately alerted to the danger of believing that humans can achieve the good life by their own efforts. For him, this was a threat to a true understanding of human nature, divine grace and the need for salvation through the death and resurrection of Christ.

About 400 there was controversy in Rome concerning death, sin and the purpose of baptism. There was hesitation in Rome concerning the doctrine associated with Cyprian and North Africa that infants are baptized not for their own sins but for the inherently sinful nature they had inherited from Adam. But was this true? How could a newborn baby be guilty of anything? Many in Rome preferred to think in terms of sinful tendencies rather than an inherently sinful nature. In North Africa the doctrine of original sin was held as the authentic tradition and would soon become orthodox belief. It could seem almost Manichaean in its pessimism about the condition in which human beings are born.

When Alaric captured Rome in 410, two of the refugees who escaped across the sea to Africa were a British monk called Pelagius and his assistant Caelestius. They arrived in Hippo at a time when Augustine was away from the town because of illness, but the absent bishop communicated with Pelagius in a kindly and courteous letter.

Opposite page:
God commanding Adam and Eve not to eat the fruit of the tree of the knowledge of good and evil. A detail from a lancet window in Chartres cathedral, France (twelfth century).

From Hippo, Pelagius continued on his way to Carthage, where Augustine claimed to have caught sight of him (he was a conspicuously big man) in May 411; but Augustine was too preoccupied with preparations for a conference to have time for a meeting. By June, when Augustine was free, Pelagius had left for Palestine. It was ironic that the two men did not meet face to face when they had the opportunity, because they were to engage in a long-range disagreement for the next 20 years.

Having been born in Britain, Pelagius went to Rome about 380, perhaps as a student of law but also to learn theology. He dedicated himself to an ascetic life, but kept in contact with the world, and is the first British-born author whose writings have survived into modern times.

Pelagius denied that human sin is inherited from Adam or that death is a consequence of Adam's disobedience. Rather, he believed that humans have a free choice to act righteously or sinfully. According to Pelagius, Adam introduced sin into the world only to the extent that he was a corrupting example. Pelagius did not attribute human sinfulness to the descent of the race from Adam, as though it were genetically inherited. He also claimed that it is possible to live a sinless life, although he admitted that not many people have done so.

In Pelagius's view, God predestines no one to righteousness or damnation, although because he is omniscient, he foresees who will believe and who will reject his grace. God forgives all who have faith in him and, once forgiven, humans have power of themselves to live lives that are pleasing to God. For this reason, Pelagius found no need for the special enabling power of the Holy Spirit. His idea of the Christian life was practically the Stoic one of ascetic self-control.

Pelagius's beliefs were particularly attractive to the wealthy aristocrats of Rome, one of whom was Caelestius

who became a leading supporter. The movement also flourished among the estate owners of Sicily. Some of Pelagius's followers held convictions rather more strongly than he did himself; among them Rufinus the Syrian, Caelestius and Julian of Eclanum.

By emphasizing human freedom to choose good by virtue of a God-given nature, Pelagius defended Christian asceticism against the charge of Manichaeism. Pelagius

himself was not concerned with the doctrine of original sin, but the concept was introduced to the movement by Rufinus, who in turn influenced Caelestius.

Augustine disagreed sharply with Pelagius's view of human nature. His own experience had given him a deep sense of human sin and hence the greatness of God's salvation. He felt that nothing less than the irresistible grace of God could have saved him from sin, and only the constant inflowing of God's grace could

An artist's
impression of
Pelagius
(c. 354–418).

sustain him in the Christian life. His Christian ideal was not Stoic self-control but love for righteousness infused by the Spirit of God.

Caelestius stayed in Carthage after Pelagius had left. He argued publicly that the baptism of infants was for sanctification in Christ rather than the remission of sins. When he offered himself for ordination to the priesthood, Paulinus of Milan (a deacon who was also a refugee from Italy) summoned him before an episcopal tribunal in the autumn of 411. Caelestius's defence provides a good outline of Pelagianism as it was emerging. He claimed that Adam died because he was mortal, not because he sinned; that human death is not the fault of Adam; nor can humans be raised to life by being identified with Christ. Caelestius's views were condemned in Carthage and he left for Ephesus where he was accepted for ordination to the priesthood.

The following year, Augustine began to preach and write against Pelagian doctrine. His first effort was prompted by an enquiry about infant baptism from the tribune and notary Marcellinus. It was Augustine's letter in reply to Marcellinus, 'On the Baptism of Infants', which he revised and issued as *On the Merits and Forgiveness of Sins and on Infant Baptism*.

Augustine had thought long and hard about the issues of infant baptism. How was baptism efficacious for a child who was unaware and unconcerned of its spiritual situation? What was the pastoral need of parents to know that their child would go to heaven? How was baptizing a child who was unconscious different from baptizing an adult who was oblivious? Ten years earlier, in *On Baptism*, Augustine had argued the importance of the faith of the parents who brought a child for baptism; now he added the need for the supporting faith of the Christian congregation, the Church.

Augustine's arguments against Pelagianism took him deep into the nature of sin. He agreed with Pelagius that it was possible for a human being to live a sinless life, but marshalled scripture and experience to deny that it had ever happened, except in the case of Jesus. Augustine argued that Jesus was unique and had assumed the appearance of sinful flesh 'for our salvation'. The rest of humankind sins because it wants to, and is inherently sinful by its physical descent from Adam.

In the early years of the debate, Augustine treated Pelagius with respect, praising him as 'a Christian of eminent virtue'. Both Augustine and Pelagius were brilliant exponents of scripture; both seeking to discern the great underlying truths and realities of the spiritual life. Augustine didn't question that the Pelagians were true believers who lived in chastity and did good works. His only criticism of them (but it was a serious one) was that they had dismissed the justice of God and substituted their own.

This was a debate about the nature of sin and its influence on human beings. For Augustine, Adam's sin was a catastrophe that rendered the human race spiritually dead. In his view the whole human race was 'in Adam' and therefore corrupt and incapable of goodness. Pelagius, in sharp contrast, believed that God had created humans with a good nature, free from sin. Sin, when it occurred, was merely an individual act or accident. It had no power to corrupt the good nature and was certainly not transmitted genetically. For Augustine this meant that Pelagius was diminishing the impact of sin and therefore the need for, and reality of, Christ's salvation.

In 412 Augustine wrote in response to a further enquiry from Marcellinus. This work was entitled *Of the Spirit and the Letter* and contrasted the Old Testament law (which worked by threat) to the New Testament 'law'

Jerome, who produced the Vulgate version of the Bible, depicted by the Flemish painter Marinus van Reymerswaele (1541), Museo del Prado, Madrid.

(which worked by faith). Pelagius had already attacked a famous phrase of Augustine's in *Confessions*, where he says to God, 'Grant what you command, and command what you will' (10.29.40). Such a sentiment implied that God's grace is paramount, in partnership with the faith of the believer, if one is to live a life without sin. Augustine was defending the centrality of grace in God's salvation, as opposed to the efforts of humans to attain godliness by legalism and ascetic practices. In God's plan of salvation, Jesus was the supreme mediator of God's grace, not merely an example of a good life.

In 415 Pelagius was accused of heresy by a young Spanish priest, Paulus Orosius, who had been sent by Augustine to Jerome at Bethlehem. Jerome had been in dispute with Pelagius for over 20 years. Pelagius succeeded in clearing himself at a diocesan synod at Jerusalem and at a provincial synod at Diospolis (Lydda),

Jerome

Jerome, Eusebius Hieronymus, was born around 345, in Strido in Dalmatia (now in Croatia). He studied Greek and Latin in Rome, was baptized at the age of 19, and became a hermit near Antioch in Syria, where he learned Hebrew and Aramaic.

Jerome's scholarship and grasp of languages made him the most learned scholar in the early Church. His urgent task was to produce a reliable version of the Bible in Latin, but the Old Testament alone took him 15 years. The result was the Vulgate version of the Bible, so called because it was in the 'vulgar' or 'common' language of Latin. Completed in 404, it was a breathtaking achievement.

Jerome had a complex personality, notorious for his bad temper and vitriolic turn of phrase. Garry Wills, describing him as 'a testy grump', says 'It was as rare for Jerome to keep a friend as for Augustine to lose one' (*St Augustine*, page 85). When he engaged in correspondence with Augustine (and on one occasion it took him nine years to reply), Jerome was sarcastic about Augustine's status both as a bishop and as a scholar.

but the African bishops condemned Pelagius and Caelestius at two councils at Carthage and Milevis in 416. They persuaded Pope Innocent I (410–17) to excommunicate them.

Caelestius went to Rome and so impressed Innocent's successor, Zosimus (417–19), that he reopened the case. The Africans stood firm and at the Council of Carthage on 1 May 418 they issued a series of nine canons in support of Augustine's doctrine of the Fall and original sin. On 30 April, the emperor Honorius (395–423), perhaps under African pressure, had issued an imperial decree denouncing Pelagius and Caelestius. Soon afterwards Pope Zosimus decided against them and by his *Epistola Tractoria* (418) reaffirmed the judgment of his predecessor. By 419 the Pelagians were banished by imperial decree. Caelestius followed Pelagius to the east, where churches were more receptive to their teaching; but in 431 they were condemned by the General Council of the Church meeting in Ephesus.

The debate with Julian

Augustine encountered more Pelagian views in a fierce and often unpleasant debate with Julian of Eclanum. Julian was confident in his convictions and dismissive of his opponents. He claimed to find the commentaries of Jerome laughable and emphasized the cultural gulf between himself as a pedigree Italian and Augustine as an African donkey. His task was to repel the African influence that was being imposed so heavy-handedly in Italy – a Punic War for theologians.

Julian suggested that Augustine's view of sin was little different from his old Manichaeism – the believer was plunged into a lifelong struggle between good and evil. Augustine held the contrary view, that Catholic Christianity avoided both the mistaken negativity of the Manichees and the false optimism of the Pelagians. Julian focused on the goodness of human nature, maintaining that those aspects of life that so concerned Augustine – such as sexual desire and death – were in fact quite natural. For Augustine, sexual desire was sinful (although it could be legitimately channelled into marriage) and the difficulties of life (and death itself) were a punishment for sin.

Julian was young enough to be Augustine's son; he was abrasive, scornful and provocative in his arguments. Augustine was an experienced controversialist, but a good deal busier than Julian – and tired. Julian was a philosopher at heart, specializing in dismissing the Manichees; whereas Augustine had moved on to the faith certainties of old age. A debate that, if conducted with more courtesy, could have yielded useful outcomes, was in

Julian of Eclanum (c. 380–454)

Julian was born in Apulia, where in 416 he succeeded his father as bishop. He came from a cultured family and was well educated, having the Greek Augustine lacked. He married a priest's daughter and was bold in his positive statements about their sexual relationship.

Julian became an enthusiastic supporter of Pelagius and attacked the *Epistola Tractora* ruling of Pope Zosimus, which had condemned Pelagius and Caelestius. In 418, at the age of 35, he led the resistance of 18 Italian bishops. As a result, he was deposed from his see and banished from Italy. He travelled in the east and was received by Theodore of Mopsuestia and Nestorius, but was expelled from both Cilicia and Constantinople.

Julian of Eclanum represented the younger generation of Pelagian believers and became the leading academic exponent of Pelagianism. Returning to the west, he settled as a teacher in Sicily. He spent half his life in exile. Three of his letters and 12 of his books are referred to by Augustine. They date from the years 418–26.

the event bad-tempered, clumsy and inconclusive. Julian in his clever scholarship was a forerunner of the Christian humanism that would reach its finest expression in Thomas Aquinas (1225–74).

Sex

Augustine has a reputation for having permanently marred the western Church's view of sex. As we have seen, Augustine as a young man had his share of sexual adventures and his mother warned him against committing adultery. As a student in Carthage he wrestled with sexual desire, seeing it as in conflict with a holy life. The Manichees required celibacy of their 'elect', but Augustine was already committed to his partner and remained a 'hearer'.

As a professor in Milan, Augustine separated from his mistress but felt the draw of 'an even deeper whirlpool of erotic indulgence' (*Confessions* 6.16.26). When he was converted in the garden in Milan, it was through reading Paul's exhortation to renounce 'debauchery and licentiousness' and 'make no provision for the flesh, to gratify its desires' (Romans 13:13, 14). From that moment he lived as a celibate, either with friends or in a monastic community.

During Augustine's debate with Julian over Pelagianism, Julian accused Augustine of wanting to destroy the institution of marriage, making his charges to the emperor Valerius, who was himself a married Christian. Augustine wrote to Valerius immediately, to deny that he was opposed to marriage and to dissociate himself from the views of Jerome, who had written vehemently of celibacy as spiritually superior to marriage.

Unfortunately, our impressions of Augustine's views on sex are shaped by his replies to Julian's sharp attacks and taunts. Augustine is forced into defensive and negative statements in order to refute his young, intellectual and witty adversary. As a result, he comes across as pessimistic about human nature, burdened with the struggle against evil and memories of sexual activity as an undertow against the stream of godliness.

In fact both Julian and Augustine shared the assumption of their age that celibacy was desirable for wholehearted consecration to God. Pelagius taught the high-minded aristocrats of Rome and Sicily that a 'sinless' life was desirable and achievable – and this entailed celibacy. Pelagius himself never married, and Julian and his wife became celibate once their marriage proved childless. By contrast, Augustine was very lax in his views that human sin is inevitable. His admissions in *Confessions* of temptation, weakness and failure were a shocking betrayal of the ascetic ideal. For Augustine, the intervention of God's grace was the only hope of holiness – hence the prayer that so outraged Pelagius: 'My entire hope is exclusively in your very great mercy. Grant what you command, and command what you will' (*Confessions* 10.29.40).

Men manoeuvring an ox-drawn water cart in a mosaic at the Roman Villa del Casale, Sicily. Early fourth century.

Augustine was rare among theologians in asserting that Adam and Eve would have enjoyed a sexual relationship in Eden: sex was a God-given part of creation, not a regrettable consequence of the Fall. Augustine agreed with Julian that if Jesus was perfect in every way then he was certainly sexually virile. The issue was not whether one had a desire and capacity for sexual activity, but how one submitted to the higher demands of holiness and godly love.

Augustine, along with many other philosophers and saints, believed that there was something chaotic and disintegrating about sex. Sex overwhelmed the soul's attempt to ascend to God by means of a disciplined, reflective and balanced life. Lust was at war with the intellect: the sex act 'throwing a man's mind from its

*'Man's maker
was made man
that He, Ruler of
the stars, might
nurse at His
mother's breast;
that the Bread
might hunger,
the Fountain
thirst, the Light
sleep, the Way be
tired on its
journey; that
Truth might be
accused of false
witness, the
Teacher be
beaten with
whips, the
Foundation be
suspended on
wood; that
Strength might
grow weak; that
the Healer might
be wounded;
that Life might
die.'*

SERMONS 191.1

tower' (*The Soliloquies* 1.17). Sexual arousal, unbidden and uncontrollable, is evidence that body and soul lack integrity of will and action. Impotency is equally evidence of an inner dividedness, as the body is unable to perform what desire and imagination demands. As all this is embarrassing, then our very sense of shame is also a result of the Fall.

It should be said in Augustine's defence that he was not obsessed with sex. He was engaged in a frank and direct argument on the issue with a frank and direct critic. So far as his other writings, sermons, letters and pastoral advice are concerned, there is no evidence that he was unhealthily preoccupied with sexual misdemeanours. He expelled a monk for a deception over the handling of property, but not for homosexuality. His own life experience meant that he was sympathetic to the struggles of others. While Pelagius and Julian made claims to perfection, Augustine was only too ready to admit human weakness in himself and his people. In his opinion, Julian was too full of youthful arrogance, but at the end of the day this was an epic debate about the very great questions of nature and grace. Like opposing boxers, Augustine and Julian traded heavy blows, but both were agreed that the fight was worthwhile.

Far from being negative about the human body or the 'lower' orders of creation, Augustine was full of affirmation and wonder for everything God has made. He eulogized about the shape and movement of the earthworm and was somewhat 'earthy' himself. He observed that the human passing of wind was 'like making music from the other end'. It was central for Augustine that God 'became flesh' in Jesus and so expressed the divine favour towards the human body with its orientations and appetites. The arduous path of bodily self-denial to achieve the soul's enlightenment was replaced by the parabola of the incarnation, whereby God reached down in Christ to restore the human race to his divinity.

Against the Arians

Another heresy that concerned Augustine was Arianism, which took its name from Arius (d. 336), a presbyter in Alexandria during the early fourth century. Between 315 and 318, Arius took issue with the sermons of his bishop, Alexander. Arius argued that Jesus was not eternal but created before the ages by the Father out of nothing. Jesus was not God but one of God's creatures, and therefore susceptible to change. Jesus was different from other creatures, and the Father bestowed dignity on him as the Son of God because of his righteousness.

Arius's ideas quickly took root and spread. In effect, he denied the eternal nature of Jesus Christ as the 'Logos' of God. In his view the Son was subordinate to, and not coequal with, the Father. The Synod of Alexandria excommunicated Arius and the Council of Nicea condemned Arianism in 325. However, the Arians achieved a wide popularity after the death of Constantine in 337, because Constantine's son and successor Constantius favoured them.

It was Athanasius, the young deacon to Alexander, who argued against Arius. Arius claimed that if Christ was 'begotten', he must have had a beginning and was therefore not eternal. Athanasius countered that to say that a father begets a child is one thing, but to say that 'the Father begat the Son' is another. One is physical and temporal, the other is eternal; one is from human will, the other from divine 'Being'. Christ, 'begotten of the Father', could not have had a beginning such as we imagine in human terms.

The questions raised by Arianism struck at the heart of the orthodox doctrines of creation, redemption and the Trinity. The Council of Nicea agreed that the Lord Jesus Christ is of one substance with the Father from eternity, as testified in the Gospel of John (John 1:1–3, 14). After Athanasius, Christ could no longer be thought of, in the Greek way, as God's intermediary in his work of creation and redemption. Athanasius insisted there is no room in

An illuminated 'I'
depicts the eagle
of John silencing
the heretic Arius
for arguing that
Jesus was not
fully divine. The
twelfth-century
Bible of
St Étienne
Harding,
Bibliothèque
Municipale,
Dijon, France.

Christian thought for any being of intermediate status between creator and creature. Redemption is an act of divine right and grace, so only God-in-Christ, and not some intermediate being, could redeem.

Athanasius carried the day and Arius was banished to Biliria. He returned to Alexandria in the closing years of his life, but was never restored to the fellowship of the Church.

Augustine's writings against the Arians are concerned to defend and clarify the trinitarian theology of the Council of Nicea. Augustine had met with Arian theology in the writings of Hilary of Poitiers and Ambrose, and in the reports of the Church councils of the late 350s. Some of his *Eighty-Three Different Questions* address Arian issues and he revisits them in his commentary on the Gospel of John and books on the Trinity.

In 418 or 419 Augustine received a copy of a collection of anti-Nicene arguments, which, although referring to Jesus Christ as Lord, emphasized his subordination to the Father. The Son was born, it was argued, in order that humanity would not despair or regard itself as worthless. Augustine wasted no time in replying. In *Against an Arian Sermon* he argues the consubstantial nature of divine Persons and defends the orthodox doctrine of the incarnation – Jesus the Son 'in the form of a servant' (John 14:28) and 'in the form of God' (John 10:30). This work was to make a distinctive contribution to the Council of Chalcedon in 451.

Almost a decade later, the Goth Sigiswulf sent an Arian bishop Maximinus to Hippo to seek peace between the two sides in the trinitarian debate. Maximinus invited Augustine to a public debate, arguing that the Father alone is the true God and that the Son, although a god, is not the true God. Augustine argued that the Son shared the same attributes as the Father. Like the Father, the Son is 'incomparable, immense, infinite, unborn, invisible'. The debate is recorded in the *Debate with Maximinus: An Arian Bishop*. When Maximinus returned to Carthage from Hippo he boasted of having won the debate. This prompted Augustine to write *Against Maximinus: An Arian* in an attempt to refute his opponent's points and strengthen his own case. In truth, Augustine's debating powers were on the wane due to his advanced age, but he still managed to refine some of the doctrinal points he had already stated in *On the Trinity*.

The Arian debate was a lengthy one, involving the exchange of many complex documents. Thanks largely

Athanasius (left) with John the Evangelist, depicted together in a wall painting.

to the efforts of Athanasius, the force of Arian teaching
was eventually dissipated, and the Nicene ruling was
confirmed at the Council of Constantinople in 381.

Against heresies
Augustine wrote other works to counter heresies. In 415
he published a treatise against some of the doctrines of
the Priscillianists and the Origenists, where he considered

them in error on the concept of 'creation from nothing' and 'eternity of punishment'. In the spring of 418 he wrote *Against Adversaries of the Law and the Prophets* to refute the old Marcionite argument that the God of the Old Testament is 'the author of war and fury' while Christ is 'the father of peace and charity'. Augustine emphasizes that the same God is revealed in the New Testament as in the Old.

In *Against the Jews* Augustine argues that the prophecies of the Old Testament have been fulfilled in Christ and the Church. He urges an attitude of humility and charity towards the Jews, but believes they are blind and stubborn and culpable for the crucifixion of Christ. He is more negative about the Jews and Judaism here than he is elsewhere, holding that the Christian Church is the new Israel and the only hope for the Jews is to convert to Christianity.

Augustine wrote a book *On Heresies* in response to a request for guidance for clergy. The request came from Quodvultdeus, a deacon and later bishop of Carthage, who wrote to Augustine in 427 or 428. Drawing on existing works and adding information from Eusebius and Jerome, Augustine discussed the nature of heresy and schism. He distinguished schism from heresy by arguing that it is persistence in schism that leads to heresy. Although the work was incomplete at the time of Augustine's death, its list of 88 heresies from Simon Magus in the Acts of the Apostles to Pelagius and Caelestius was valued by the African clergy as an authoritative work in the early Middle Ages.

Greatest Writings and Old Age

In 386, during the happy interlude of living in community at the rural retreat of Cassiciacum, Augustine had devised a new kind of writing. Part personal exploration and part prayer, he penned *The Soliloquies*. Many years later, as a bishop looking back on his life (and to some extent protecting his reputation), he embarked on a unique journey of the soul – the story of his life, as told to God, that is *Confessions*. In what is effectively the first autobiography, he explores the mystery of himself as an expression of the mystery of God. This, in turn, led him to write another great book about the nature of God: *On the Trinity*.

The Confessions

The *Confessions*, one of Augustine's greatest and most original works, was written between 397 and 401, that is, soon after the author had become bishop of Hippo and when some of his critics were concerned about his Manichaean past. The title betrays the dual nature of the work. In one sense confession is the avowal of sins, and Augustine's *Confessions* is the first work to examine in detail the interior state of the mind. The Donatists accused Augustine of remaining a crypto-Manichaean and the first nine books are autobiographical, describing Augustine's loss of faith, the ten years of adherence to Mani, succeeded by deep scepticism and a conversion to Neoplatonism that led to the recovery of his childhood faith and baptism. The facts of Augustine's boyhood and youth are better known perhaps than any in late antiquity.

Much of *Confessions* is expressed in terms of the utmost praise to God. Augustine exults that he was so graciously turned from his futile and tortured way of living when he read from Romans in the Milanese garden. He rejoices in the vision he shared with his mother at Ostia before her death. Having turned the corner from paganism to Christianity, Augustine then proceeds to write about creation, memory, time and the Trinity. The key to the entire work, which includes Augustine's past and his move towards God, may be found in the first few lines of the work: 'You have made us for yourself and our heart is restless until it rests in you.' The work in its entirety is a description of the theme of return to and rest in God. The *Confessions* may be interpreted as a Christian counterpart to the pagan *Odyssey* of Homer. In this work on past faults, conversion and salvation, we may find a variety of themes and interpretations. Many of these find their roots in the pagan past. The fall and return of the soul to God is found in Plotinus and Porphyry and in the parable of the prodigal son. The search for and the discovery of truth is found in both Cicero and the Gospel of Matthew. It is, perhaps, the grounding of one man's ascent to God that has made the work so engaging to such a variety of readers throughout the ages; a patristic everyman.

By revisiting his past, sometimes with great wrestling and difficulty, to capture the truth of a situation, Augustine believed he would discover the mystery of God within himself. This in turn led Augustine into an exploration of the nature of memory, which gave him an analogy for God's creation of time out of eternity. The whole creation was present in God's eternity and only became a physical reality when it was pronounced in time by his 'Word'. Time, in turn, is a processing of the future into the past, moving through a point that is immeasurable, for no sooner is it present than it is gone. Yet we only know the past as a present memory and the future as a present anticipation!

'For you are the
abiding light
by which I
investigated all
these matters
whether they
existed, what
they were, and
what value
should be
attached to
them. I listened
to you teaching
me and giving
instructions…
I can find no safe
place for my soul
except in you.'

CONFESSIONS 10.40.65

The central panel
of an Italian
triptych depicting
the Holy Trinity,
with Romuald
and John the
Evangelist.
Nardo di Cione
(died c. 1365),
Galleria
dell'Accademia,
Florence.

In these abstruse reflections, Augustine was exploring the mystery that was himself as a clue to the nature of God in whose 'image' he was made. He finds himself both 'in' time and somehow outside it. In these and other speculations he shows himself a forerunner of disciplines as diverse as psychology and particle physics. The ideas tumble onto the page, so agog is he with the joy of exploration and the wonder of discovery.

As the century turned, Augustine's thoughts focused in three main areas: the human mind, time and eternity, and the triune God. He devoted separate books to each at the end of *Confessions*: Book 11 on time and memory; Book 12 on Genesis; and Book 13 on the Trinity. The three works form a meditation on the Persons of the Trinity: the Father creating time, the Word articulating the world, and the Spirit binding all together in love. From this perspective, the first ten books of *Confessions* were a preface to the three at the end, as Augustine explored his own Genesis and Fall in autobiographical episodes of theft, nakedness and grief.

In the course of his writing, Augustine was forging an understanding of the will that was new to philosophy. In Neoplatonic thought the highest human faculty was the intellect, and wrongdoing was explained as a mistaken self-interest. Now Augustine introduces the will as a force to be reckoned with – in the case of Satan, a high intellect lacking love. By contrast, in Augustine's trinitarian

'Love is the act of a lover and the love given the loved person. It is a trinity: the lover, the loved person, and the love itself.'

ON THE TRINITY 8.14

theology, God's free will is 'loving love'.

In the light of his developing thought, Augustine recast the account of his conversion. In *Confessions* it becomes less an intellectual transition to a higher plain of thought, as in the *Cassiciacum Dialogues*, and more a triumph of God's grace over his pride. In retrospect, Monica's prayers have a more significant role to play than the philosophical arguments of Manlius Theodorus.

In *First Meanings in Genesis*, Augustine explores a 'fundamental' meaning of the text – not in terms of a literal interpretation, but in terms of its primary, foundational sense. The 'light' that God creates on the 'first day' is not that of the sun (which was created on the fourth day) but something more subtle. Terms such as 'light' and 'day' in the Genesis narrative are to convey divine realities to human minds. The 'light' of the first 'day' is the beginning of the process of intelligibility whereby human beings may eventually apprehend the works of God. One day 'the true light, which enlightens everyone' will come into the world (John 1:9). We know God because the mystery of our intellect reveals God's mystery.

In *On the Trinity*, Augustine draws on his own perceptions of himself as 'trinitarian'. For example, he can perceive time and memory in three ways: as past, present and future. He finds that his soul has three distinct and complementary faculties: the will (to act), the intellect (to articulate reality) and the memory (to establish continuity and identity). These, for Augustine, are glimpses of the mystery of God, who is Father, Word (or Son), and Spirit. Augustine's perceptions were to shape western theology for a thousand years – not only in their conclusions, but in their observant, reflective and astonishingly honest quest for truth.

The fall of Rome
In 410 Alaric the Visigoth captured Rome. For 620 years the city had been impregnable, but now the invading

hordes swept in – the first since Hannibal's surprise invasion across the Alps.

Alaric was an Arian Christian who spared the Church's treasures. The wider empire continued to function, as the emperors of east and west ruled from their courts at Constantinople and Ravenna respectively. But in truth the conquest was a profound shock – and compelling evidence that the old order was disintegrating.

The fall of Rome was not just a crisis for pagans, but also for Christians. They had thought of their faith redeeming the empire and establishing Rome as 'the eternal city'. Now they found themselves blamed for Rome's fall, because they had offended the pagan deities who had protected the city for so long.

Many Christians fled to Africa as refugees. Augustine welcomed those who arrived in Hippo and listened to their questions and doubts. Why had Rome fallen? Did its ruin mean that civilization itself had failed and the end of the world was at hand? He turned the issues in his mind and began to formulate an answer.

'Rome, capturer of the world, fell captive.'

JEROME, C. 345–419

The City of God

Augustine's finest apologetic work, *City of God*, is also one of the great masterpieces of Christian literature. It was begun in 412 and not completed until 427, although books from it were published at intervals during this period. The work as a whole follows a clear structure. It is divided into two main parts. The first ten books are a refutation of the full teachings of the pagans. Books 11–22 are a demonstration and defence of the truth of the Christian faith and are presented as a positive counterpart to the negative criticisms voiced in the first part of the book.

In the first part, Augustine refutes the worship of pagan gods, whether for personal happiness, imperial supremacy, or hope of an afterlife. He demolishes pagan religion as it is variously presented – 'mythical', 'civil', or 'natural'.

In the second part, Augustine expounds the idea that all humanity lives in one of two cities: the city of God, symbolized by Jerusalem, or the earthly city, symbolized by Babylon. In three sections, he deals with the origin, development and end of these two cities. They are not like earthly cities with geographical locations and boundaries. Rather, they are mystical cities, whose citizenship is not determined by birthplace or family line, but by the object of a person's love or the goal of their actions.

Augustine was concerned to dethrone Rome from its idealized place in the popular mind. It had been defeated many times in its history, and there was no reason to lay the blame for its most recent fall at the Church's door. Christianity had not undermined its sense of citizenship or its will to resist enemies. Far from subverting patriotism, the Church reinforced it – both the Old and New Testaments command allegiance to civil authority and the laws of one's country. Similarly, by censuring pagan practices, Christianity had strengthened the moral fibre of the community and promoted the peace and prosperity of the city.

The fall of Rome was a time for prophetic insight. Augustine was saying that Rome was never the city that could satisfy human hearts. Only the city of God could do that.

The dream of a 'Christian era' had been dashed, but Augustine offered a greater perspective, an enduring identity. He addressed the bewildered refugees in Carthage as 'God's own people, the body of Christ'; the 'citizens of Jerusalem' who belonged to a better place.

Because the two 'cities' of human belonging and loyalty, 'Jerusalem' and 'Babylon', are inextricably mixed in this world, Augustine encouraged Christians to demonstrate their distinctiveness. They should long for God's future and perceive in the changes forced upon them an opportunity for growth. Of those who had been killed, injured, assaulted or dispossessed, he emphasized that no physical accident could affect the security of their souls; no material loss could rob them of their eternal inheritance in heaven. He especially urged those women who had been raped not to take their own lives because of their shame.

Augustine had been raised on the heroic story of Virgil's *Aeneid*, in which the gods ordain that Rome will model the divine order of justice. Now he counters that Rome could never do such a thing. Only the city of God is perfectly ordered and at peace. The human state, like the Church, contains a mixture of good and bad, saints and sinners. In saying this, Augustine sails close to the old divisions of Manichaeism, where good and evil are

John the Divine is granted a vision of the Heavenly Jerusalem. The Abingdon Apocalypse, English illuminated manuscript (c. 1270–75).

The bishop as judge

As bishop of Hippo, Augustine was required to rule on many issues. In 411 a particularly difficult episode centred on a man called Pinian who was a wealthy refugee from Rome. The congregation at Hippo wanted to seize on him to make him their priest – perhaps because he had considerable landholdings locally. Pinian escaped only by promising to live in Hippo and not to accept ordination elsewhere. But the promise was made under duress and he fled. Augustine's task was to deal justly with both sides. He told his congregation he would resign if they forced ordination on Pinian; but he also felt strongly that Pinian should have kept his promise!

Augustine was becoming accustomed to wielding a weighty opinion. In his ecclesiastical court, he upheld sound principles and took the opportunity to demonstrate a quality of mercy that he felt the Romans often lacked. Since Constantine's conversion, the legislative functions of Church and State had begun to overlap – bishops presided in civil courts and emperors summoned ecclesiastical councils. As religious intolerance was the order of the day, Catholics, Donatists and Arians took it in turns to oust each another from positions of privilege, depending on the views of the emperor in power or the local group in political ascendancy.

Despite his desire for leniency in some civil cases, Augustine developed a justification for religious suppression. He declined to punish the conscience of others with torture or execution, but nevertheless felt that the law should 'compel' heretics to arrive at an orthodox faith for their own good. Had not the beggars in the highways and hedges been 'compelled' to come in to the Master's banquet in Luke's parable (Luke 14:23)? Augustine may have been using the law for the purpose of love, but in so doing he placed a cruel legal precedent in the hands of his successors; not least the perpetrators of religious persecution in future generations.

'Let the heretics be drawn from the hedges… use compulsion outside, so freedom can arise once they are inside.'

SERMONS 112.8

Augustine is
blessed by an
angel but
distracted by
devils as he
writes, in this
woodcut from a
French edition of
the *City of God*.

continuously at war. But he explains that the earthly city
is not all bad, as even wicked people display virtues of
courage and have good motives to care for their own. To
resolve this, he borrows from the Donatist theologian
Tyconius, to explain that the conflict is moving towards a
final resolution – the harvest and judgment of God at the
end of the age.

Augustine challenges the classical theory of Cicero
(and Plato before him) that a state is based on mutual
self-interest and an agreed standard of justice. Instead,
he emphasizes the primacy of the will over the intellect
and of love over justice. He formulated a view of
the earthly city that admitted, and worked with,
imperfections such as unjust regimes and criminal

elements. Even in an imperfect setting, he urged
Christians to be good citizens and required officials to
be impartial.

In answer to the question 'Who then belongs to the
City of God?' Augustine admits we don't know. Only God

knows – indeed, in Augustine's opinion, God *foreknows*. In this world, as in the parable, wheat and weeds grow together. Unlike the parable, by God's grace, 'weeds' can become 'wheat'. Augustine's image here is not of an indissoluble boundary between Church and State, but

The fall of Rome depicted in violent storm and human brutality in an oil painting by Thomas Cole: *The Course of Empire: Destruction* (1836), New York Historical Society, New York.

rather a fluid, changing, dynamic process of spiritual transaction and transformation.

Miracles

One unexpected development of Augustine's later thought was his conversion to the reality of miracles. At one time he had tended to deny them as part of his adamant opposition to the cults of the martyrs that were centred on eucharistic feasts and prayers at their tombs. But when there was a fresh wave of miracles in Africa in the 420s, Augustine came to admit that such divine interventions were possible. A God who could take on human form could surely make creative intrusions in human lives. In taking this position, he was also making a concession to the charismatic faith and fervour of the Donatists, who were now 'officially' reunited with the Catholic Church and for whom the miraculous was a normal expectation.

Reconsiderations

As Augustine moved into his seventies, he realized that his energy and time were beginning to run out. After his old friend Severus died, who had been bishop of Milevis (Mila) for 30 years, Augustine began to put his own house in order. He nominated his colleague Eraclius as his successor and delegated to him some of his episcopal functions, such as the hearing of court cases. He used the time thus gained to put in hand a review and revision of his own writings.

Augustine recognized that his thought had developed over the course of his lifetime and that he did not now necessarily agree with some of the views of his younger self. He had taken care to retain copies of each of his books in the library of the monastery at Hippo, and he now sat down to reread, amend and place in chronological order, the complete works. He also wrote a reflection on them that he entitled *Reconsiderations*, by which he meant a reconsideration rather than a

withdrawal of his opinions. He also intended to do
the same with his letters and sermons, but he was
interrupted by a fresh avalanche of correspondence from
Julian of Eclanum. One unexpected benefit of this huge
and unprecedented task was the discovery and
completion of his great work *On Christian Doctrine*,
which had lain unfinished since 397. Shortly after
Augustine's death his friend and pupil, Possidius, also
made a catalogue that included the letters and sermons
but he, too, was aware that even his catalogue was not
complete. It is a measure of Augustine's reputation and
standing that in the Middle Ages many works were falsely
attributed to him. Modern scholarship has, to a large
extent, determined those works that are authentically
Augustine and others that are pseudo-Augustine. In the
second half of the last century many additional letters

Talking to Boniface

In 417 a Christian official called Boniface was appointed
as commander ('Count') of the Roman army in Africa.
Remembering, no doubt, his close co-operation with
Marcellinus, Augustine first wrote to Boniface and then
journeyed 120 miles to speak with him.

Augustine urged Boniface that war should only be
waged when it was necessary to secure peace, and with the
minimum force necessary for success. In dealings with an
enemy, it was appropriate to act with truth and mercy, and
without resort to the death penalty.

For his part, Boniface confided in Augustine his intention
to become a monk. The bishop went to great lengths (hence
the 120 miles) to dissuade the army commander from
relinquishing the godly vocation of protecting a Christian
peace.

and sermons that were written by Augustine were discovered and these have now been added to the catalogue.

To a large extent Augustine's works are the product of a man who was converted first to philosophy and second to Christianity, a man who was ordained bishop within a century of Christianity being recognized by the emperor, and a man who was a teacher and a monk. Augustine's early interest in philosophy is mirrored in his first works. His dissatisfaction with the Manichees led to many polemical writings against these and other heretics. His desire to defend the faith against pagans resulted in his apologetic works and within a few years of beginning these he naturally turned to teaching and producing dogmatic writings. As a newly consecrated bishop Augustine wrote a short series of moral and pastoral books. His turning away from Manichaeism to Christianity and, thereafter, his continual study of the Bible resulted in his exegetical writings. As a monk Augustine wrote some of the earliest monastic rules in the medieval west. Reflection on his early life in his mid-forties resulted in one of the earliest autobiographical works in Christian literature. For over 40 years (from the winter of 386 until his death in 430), Augustine also was an extremely productive letter writer and some 300 letters have so far been discovered. As a priest and then bishop Augustine delivered over 400 sermons and these, together with the letters, reflect not only Augustine's own life and teaching but also the world in which he lived and worked.

Last days

As Augustine laboured in the library at Hippo, the storm clouds of war gathered around Roman Africa. Boniface, the 'Count' with whom Augustine had previous dealings, had now become sadly corrupted by his power and distracted by political machinations in Italy. He had allowed the soldiers under his command to become brutal and undisciplined, and left the province vulnerable to marauding tribes from the Sahara. Augustine wrote, carefully and confidentially, to rebuke him.

But there was another threat to the security of Africa. In May 429, the barbarian Vandals – 80,000 men, women and children, swelled by Alans and Goths and led by the Arian chief Gaiseric – crossed from Europe by the Straits of Gibraltar. They moved slowly east towards Hippo, meeting with little resistance. Roman rule in Africa was in a state of collapse. As successive Numidian towns fell to the invader, Boniface attempted to strengthen the fortifications of Hippo and there decided to make his stand. The Christian bishops and their congregations came for refuge as Gaiseric set up a blockade from the sea and embarked on a lengthy siege. In the third month of the siege Augustine fell ill, and on 28 August 430, he died. He was almost 76.

One of Augustine's last pieces of pastoral advice was that pastors who were able to flee the invading Vandals

A Vandal rides triumphant, with a Christian symbol branded on his horse's flank. A detail from a Roman mosaic made in Carthage c. AD 500, now in the British Museum, London.

‚M ADMODVM INOBITV BEATI AVGVSTINI AQVAMPLVRIMIS EIVS

INCELIS COMITANTIBVS ANGELIS FERRI VISA E

The funeral of
Augustine
imagined by
Benozzo Gozzoli
(1420–97),
a Florentine
painter
who trained
under
Fra Angelico.
From the Church
of Sant'Agostino,
San Gimignano,
Italy.

*'Those who have
need of others
must not be
abandoned by
those whom they
need.'*

LETTERS 228.2

*'He is no great
man who thinks
it a great thing
that sticks and
stones should
fall, and that
men, who must
die, should die.'*

ENNEADS 1.4.7

should stay with the helpless members of their churches.

Augustine was probably buried in his cathedral, the Basilica Paci. His remains were later transported to Sardinia and from there, around the year 725, to Pavia, where they rest in the basilica of San Pietro in Ciel d'Oro. As to his precious books, it seems that when Hippo eventually fell to the Vandals, it did so without too much damage to the town or Augustine's library. Possidius, bishop of Calama, had spent the remaining months of the siege cataloguing the works, which were transported in later years to the apostolic library in Rome.

**Augustine's final
resting place: his
tomb in San
Pietro in Ciel
d'Oro, Pavia,
Italy.**

As far as Augustine could guess, his life's work might be dying with him. The Roman order that had held sway throughout Africa during his lifetime was being swept away. The structure and continuity of the Church's worship, churches, services and sacraments were in ruins. In the face of such a demolition, he drew deeply from the dispassionate perspective of Plotinus.

Legacy

Augustine died in 430, having lived all but five years of his life in Roman North Africa. For the last 34 years he was bishop of Hippo, a port that is now Annaba in Algeria. His town was not significant, nor was his office (there were 500 bishops in Africa), yet his influence has been monumental on all subsequent generations. He is well called a 'doctor of the Church' – a learned, sound and saintly defender, exponent and propagator of the Christian faith. The other 'doctors' of this age in the western Church are Ambrose, Gregory the Great and Jerome; but Augustine stands head and shoulders above them in his intellectual influence, which continues to the present day.

Gregory 1 (540–604), known as 'the Great', in his study. An illumination from the Duc de Berry's 'Book of Hours'. Bibliothèque Nationale, Paris.

Augustine is remembered in the popular mind for his dramatic conversion to the Christian faith. Along with Saul on the Damascus Road and John Wesley in the church in Aldersgate Street in London, Augustine in the garden hearing a child's voice calling, 'Pick up and read, pick up and read', has lodged in the Church's memory as a classic example of an individual turning to God. Other enduring images, of his devout mother, Monica, his riotous youth and his years living with a mistress and child, have also struck chords, both censorious and sympathetic, in the hearts and circumstances of subsequent generations. Here, in Augustine, is a real person struggling with real life.

But Augustine's life and circumstances would be of little enduring importance were it not for the

'Who are you, Lord?' Saul of Tarsus is converted to become the Apostle Paul as he journeys to persecute the followers of Christ in Damascus (Acts 9). An engraving by Gustav Doré from Doré's Bible (1866).

extraordinary greatness of his intellect and the quality and influence of his writing. Augustine's questing, enquiring mind, was central to his achievement. Nothing seems to have been outside the scope of his interest and observation, from the kicking of a baby to the origins of time. Today he might have been a professor of philosophy, a research psychologist or a particle physicist and, in his spare time, a newspaper columnist or spin doctor.

Long before the advent of the printing press (to say nothing of electronic communication), Augustine produced and distributed dozens of profoundly influential books and wrote hundreds of letters. In addition, nearly 400 of his sermons were recorded by the shorthand

writers who attended him. His output of more than
5 million words is greater than that of any other ancient
author; two of his works, the *Confessions* and *City of God*
must rank among the all-time 'greats' of world literature.

Augustine's work constitutes a vital stage of
development in western thought, integrating the insights
and principles of Greek philosophy with Christian theology,
and establishing the orthodox faith in the face of several
vigorous heresies. What were the key aspects of
Augustine's thought?

Sigmund Freud,
the pioneering
psychologist
famous for his
exploration of
the subconscious.
A drawing by
Ferdinand
Schmutzer
(1870–1928)
when Freud
was 80.

A modern man

We know more about the life and character of
Augustine than of anyone else in the ancient
world. He profoundly shaped the western way of
thinking about humanity and God. In this we find
him speaking across the centuries with an almost
contemporary voice. His *Confessions* not only
constitute a new form of literature (really the
first autobiography), but begin to chart the unseen
continent of the 'subconscious' mind, which is now the
province of psychology. Here, with a startling degree of
honesty and self-awareness, is an ancient stretch of a road
that leads to Descartes, Pepys and Freud.

He wrote over a period of almost half a century,
addressing a wide range of issues, and often responding to
the controversies that raged in his time. It is not surprising
to find that his ideas changed and developed. Augustine
himself learned as he wrote; he was, in his own words,
'a man who writes as he progresses and who progresses
as he writes'.

Good and evil

A key issue for Augustine was the origin and nature of
evil. At first Augustine accepted the dualistic beliefs of the
Manichees, that there is a battle raging between good and
evil, and that pure 'spirit' is entombed in the degraded
substance of 'matter'. Later, he came to believe that

'matter' is part of the One God's good creation, affirmed and dignified in the incarnation of Christ (the 'Word made flesh'). He came to see evil as the consequence of humans wrongly using their God-given free will.

Augustine's ideas were often forged in the heat of debate. Not only the Manichees, but also the Donatists and the Pelagians engaged him in lengthy and testing controversy. But long-term his heart was in the questions of the great philosophers, concerning the nature of happiness, knowledge and choice; or seeking a definition of God and the human condition. Here he engaged his own great intellect with the giants of classical thought. (It is interesting to note in passing that even the word 'heart' used in this way was coined by Augustine.)

A Christian Platonism

Augustine came to a settled conviction of his own beliefs through encounters with Neoplatonist thinkers in Milan, especially Ambrose. Neoplatonism opened up the dimension of spirit beyond space and time. This, together with the extraordinary story of Antony of Egypt's devotion to God and the challenge of Paul's letter to the Romans, liberated Augustine into an informed and spacious faith, secure in mind and morals. He himself then became the key thinker in forging a synthesis between Christianity and the classical philosophy of Plato and Aristotle. Plotinus had done the foundational work for this (although he was not himself a Christian), which Augustine both critiqued and developed. Augustine's work effectively forms a bridge between the ancient, medieval and modern worlds.

Augustine liked the 'dialogue' form of writing, which reflected the question and answer of conversation and debate. In this he carried the enquiring style of Plato and Cicero into Christian education. Augustine's *Christian Teaching* is a supremely influential work, in which he outlines a Christian approach to learning and study, with permission both to draw on secular insights and to explore scripture as allegory. It is the first work of its kind, in east or west, to set out a Christian approach to meaning, exposition, understanding and persuasion. In writing it, Augustine shaped the way in which the Christian faith has been taught ever since.

Original sin

Augustine concluded that sin is a wilful misdirection of love. For him, love should be properly and completely offered to God, and all human desires (which are accessed through the physical senses and worldly ambition) are to be rigorously subjected to the higher love of God.

For Augustine, evil is a subversion or corruption of the original order of creation. This corruption has resulted in the disease and death that are now an inescapable part of human experience. Although God can use these afflictions to curb human pride and punish wickedness, the fact is that without sin there would be no need for such discipline. While the Manichees had located evil in 'matter' (the stuff of which we are made), Augustine identified the crucial role of the 'will' (our essential desire and motivation). From this he developed a profound and enduring psychology of sin.

Aristotle teaching his students. The great Greek philosopher (384–322 BC) is seen through Turkish eyes in this thirteenth-century illustration on vellum from 'The Better Sentences and Most Precious Dictions' by Seljuk Al-Moubbachir. The Topkapi Palace Museum, Istanbul, Turkey.

Si sai uous uer icu priet · Eu meine
la gile a ada fet · Cauint estoit
en cel mointe · E out ada t eue lesse ·
Uuint le deable t a eue dit · kreste
ceo q deu defendit · le fruit q ee
en ce pomer · Est tute sa force t son poer ·
Pren la pumne si la mangez · E can

ke il feet uo sarez · Eue de
ceu estoit tro feble · E
mestenant ele ciu le
deble · Ele pst la pu
me t la mordist · Eada
de la mejn · la pnt son
angel tu mestenant
viuit

If sin is essentially a turning away from God to love lesser things, then Augustine saw no need to look further for an origin of evil. The experience of stealing pears as a youth had led him to distinguish between sin and a crime. A crime was the form sin might take, but sin itself was the desire for something other than the love of God: in thieving pears, this was nothing more than the compulsion to be accepted by his friends. Augustine traced this tendency back to the Fall, when Adam preferred the companionship of Eve to the company of God. This tendency, inherited by all descendants of Adam and Eve, means that sin is 'original' to human nature.

Augustine developed his doctrine of original sin in response to Pelagius, who held that a person can live a good life by his or her own effort. Augustine believed, on the contrary, that humans have no choice but to sin, because their sinful disposition is inherited from Adam and Eve. Adam and Eve had choice and therefore the freedom not to sin, but their descendants can change only with a special dispensation of God's grace. It was Augustine's prayer of complete dependence on God ('Grant what you command, and command what you will', *Confessions*) that stirred Pelagius to argue for human free will and moral responsibility. This did not mean that Pelagius viewed human nature as perfect, but he believed that humans have a capacity to change themselves with the help of the God-given grace with which they are born. His stance was in line with the classical Stoicism that had given dignity, courage and self-reliance to the Roman age.

But Augustine disagreed. Instead, he drew on his own experience of God's special grace. Without such grace he was sure he could never have been saved from his sinful life. Without God's grace, a person can never make even the first move towards a change of life. The ongoing life of faith and goodness is likewise dependent on a continuous outpouring of this same divine grace. For Augustine, God's grace must be both 'prevenient' (to enable one to turn to

'The fault is not in our stars but in ourselves.'

WILLIAM SHAKESPEARE, *JULIUS CAESAR* II.134

Opposite page: **Adam and Eve are deceived by the serpent and banished from paradise (Genesis 3). An English manuscript illumination from the Holkham Bible Picture Book (c. 1327–35).**

God in the first place) and 'concomitant' (to enable one to continue in a Christian way of life). In an age when those who had been martyred were praised as the 'elect', Augustine wanted every Christian to know the grace of God, whether they were male or female, celibate or married.

Augustine pointed to the Church's practice of infant baptism as evidence of original sin. Why baptize an innocent child, unless it already has an inherently sinful nature? This, he argued, indicates that sin springs not from human choice but from the fallen nature inherited from Adam.

The Church has followed Augustine in asserting the necessity of supernatural grace to overcome the inherent resistance of human nature to the love of God. Augustine went further, to argue that God's grace is irresistible; a doctrine that found a valued place in Calvin's doctrine in the sixteenth century, but not in the wider orthodoxy of the Church.

Salvation

Augustine's understanding of salvation centres entirely on Christ. Jesus Christ is the God-man, who is the perfect mediator because he is both human divinity and divine humanity. He is the perfect mediator because he is both priest and sacrifice. Christ mediates between a holy, just and immortal God and sinful, unjust and mortal humans, to bring them from death to life, from disintegration to unity, from sin to salvation. This is the reason Christ came – to save human beings from sin and death. There is no other Saviour or way of salvation, but Christ alone who reconciles the whole world back to God.

It is because Christ came to reconcile humankind to God that Augustine deduced there has been a separation from God through sin. And because Christ died for all, Augustine deduced that all are tainted by this 'original' sin. With Paul, Augustine can say that sin has come through Adam and salvation has come through Christ.

Grace

For Augustine, God's grace is all-important for God's work in the world and in spiritual creatures (by which he means angels and humans). It is by grace that humans are moved to know and love God.

Augustine followed the Neoplatonists in thinking of God's power and love being emanated from the highest orders of being to the lowest. Adapted into a Christian frame of reference, angels and humans are enlightened and empowered by turning towards the Word of God, Jesus Christ. To turn away from the Word is to lapse into sin and futility. Again, it is by the continuing work of God's grace that angels and humans can live and move and have their being in the light and love of God.

In Augustine's understanding, grace is not something God has created, but rather the very presence and action of God in human life. The Spirit of God is constantly, eternally, proceeding from the Father and the Son, and being bestowed on God's creatures in time and place. Even devils and the damned receive this emanation, which is manifested in such light, sound judgment and desire for fulfilment as they have. Without the grace of God, which is the sustaining life-giving power and love of the Word, creation would collapse into nothingness. The struggle Paul describes as taking place within him, between the good he wants to do and the evil he actually does, is an example of the Holy Spirit drawing the individual to a higher life.

Sex

Augustine is widely suspected of disapproving of sex, except in the context of marriage and for the necessity of having children. He has long been blamed for a range of mistaken attitudes to sex, from denial or rejection to guilt and shame. In fact he was a moderate voice in the context of his time, when both pagan philosophers and ascetic Christians were advocating celibacy as the way to a higher life.

Of Augustine's ascetic contemporaries, Jerome likened marriage to a tangled thornbush (confusing, uncomfortable, but occasionally fruitful) while Gregory of Nyssa thought sexuality was an unfortunate bestial addition despoiling humanity's originally 'angelic' nature. Augustine, by contrast, was ready to affirm human sexuality in its physical, psychological and spiritual dimensions. He challenged Julian of Eclanum to contemplate the wonderful sex Adam and Eve must have enjoyed in the Garden of Eden. Sex and sexuality were not results of the Fall, but a vital part of God's original and perfect creation.

As a writer and pastor, Augustine treated sex with caution. He knew something of its complexities and pain in his own life. He advised that sexual relations should take place within the discipline of marriage and for the purpose of having children, but he declined to make sex for pleasure a very great misdemeanour. For him, sexual relations were disappointing in the sense that the Fall had spoiled and diminished every aspect of human life. Everything could have been so much better as God intended.

Scripture

Augustine approached scripture as God's truth, even if he had to begin by correcting the translation or challenging the accuracy of a manuscript. He worked his theology from scripture, seeing in it the authority of Christ himself, backed by the consistent witness of the Church. He argued for the unity of the Bible's message through themes such as original sin and redemption, grace and free will.

Over the years, Augustine expounded scripture in a variety of ways, never bound by any one formula in his approach. As a bishop, he was first and foremost a preacher and teacher, and invariably he started from the scriptures. In the letter to the Romans Augustine found God's justice, mercy and predestination. In the Gospel and first letter of John he found an emphasis on God's love. But his first and favourite explorations seem to have been in the book of Genesis, the Psalms and Paul's letters, and it is these to which he returned time and again.

If Augustine enjoyed an allegorical approach in illuminating the Bible for a mixed congregation of listeners, he always addressed the literal sense intended by the original authors when he came to his doctrinal studies and commentaries.

The mystery of God

Much of what Augustine wrote was in response to the controversies of his day. An exception to this was his work *On the Trinity*, which he wrote in 15 volumes, starting in 399 and continuing over some 20 years. In it he laid the foundation for trinitarian theology.

The Council of Constantinople in 381 had rejected two extremes of understanding of the Godhead: the Arian view that the Son is subordinate to the Father, and therefore not God in the same sense as the Father is; and the one taught by Sabellius, that the terms 'Father', 'Son' and 'Spirit' are merely descriptions of three modes in which we perceive the activity of the indivisible One. The orthodox doctrine of the Trinity took its stand between these poles, asserting that God is both one and three at the same time.

Augustine understood God in terms of a triple nature – supreme Being, first Truth and eternal Love. To him it was obvious that a 'trinitarian' nature is part of everyday experience, for human beings are themselves a complexity and unity of body, mind and spirit. Augustine discerned three aspects in particular – believing, knowing and willing – that are united in a single personality. But he found several others: memory, intelligence and will; mind, knowledge and love; the lover, the beloved and the love that binds them.

Establishing that 'three-in-one-ness' as part of every human's self-understanding was relatively straightforward.

'It is better that you should understand me in my barbarism, than that you should be flooded by my fluency.'

EXPLANATIONS OF THE PSALMS 36.3.6

Christ
Pantokrator
(Ruler of All),
depicted in
mosaic in the
dome of the
Katholikon
(Church) of the
Monastery at
Daphni, near
Athens (eleventh
century).

*'God is
everything
which He has
except for the
relations by
which each
person is related
to another. There
is no doubt that
the Father has
the Son, but the
Father is not the
Son...'*

CITY OF GOD 11.10.1

But this still understood the Trinity in terms of a metaphor of human personality. How, then, to understand the idea of division within the Godhead? Augustine found the talk of three 'persons' unhelpful, and preferred to think in terms of *relationships*. Within the Trinity, the Father is the fount or principle of Godhead, the Son is eternally begotten and the Spirit eternally proceeds.

Augustine identified the Holy Spirit as proceeding from the Father and the Son as from a single principle. We see again the influence of Platonism on his thought. But the Father, who is the fount or origin of the divinity, has conceded it to the Son to emanate the Holy Spirit. The Spirit emanates or proceeds as love, which is an inclination and gift of communion. Here Augustine draws a model from psychology: 'the will (love) proceeds from the intellect but not as the image of the intellect' (*On the Trinity* 15.27.50). He distinguishes between 'generation' and 'procession', with the example that 'it is not the same thing to see with the intellect as to desire and enjoy with the will' (*On the Trinity* 15.27.50).

Augustine's writings on the Trinity are original, daring,

brilliant and profound. He closes the chapter on Origen's influence, which had made the Son and Spirit subordinate to the Father, and opens instead a relational understanding, subtle, mutual and reciprocal, which has been taken up by all the great Christian traditions.

The mystery of humanity

At the centre of Augustine's understanding of humanity is that we are created in the image of God. For Augustine, the image of a person comes from within – from the mind rather than the body – and is inseparable from the immortality of the soul. This image of God in us is deformed through sin, but can be restored by grace. Humans have been made for God and are being restored to fellowship with God. This is the foundation of Augustine's Christian self-understanding.

Humanity is not only created in God's image but is also enlightened by God's truth. 'Our illumination is a participation in the Word, that is, in that life which is the Light of men' (*On the Trinity* 4.2.4). God is not only the source of our being but the light of our understanding, which Augustine describes as 'the sun of the soul'. For Augustine, a happy life is one that enters into the joy of God's truth, which is God's wisdom. This introduces an important sense of development, journey and hope into human existence that is distinctively Christian, both for individuals and the Church. We are held together and our lives move forward in the love and providence of God; our sense of history derives from this faith.

'You have made us for yourself and our heart is restless until it rests in you.'

CONFESSIONS 1.1.1

The elect

Augustine was clear that only a proportion of the human race would be saved. Part of the evidence was that while some believers joined the 'elect' by martyrdom, others were clearly damned by taking the side of the persecutors. Again, many people were passing through life without being baptized, which in the African Church was considered essential for salvation. Augustine followed

Cyprian in insisting that 'outside the Church there is no salvation'; but even so he claimed no certain knowledge as to who was saved and who was damned.

The Christian Church is a mixture of saints and sinners, some being led to salvation and some being tolerated until they are separated out and thrown away. Augustine was all too aware of the danger of damnation, which he saw as a reflection of God's justice. But God is also loving and merciful, and Augustine believed that he has predestined some people to salvation and the life of heaven. He did not make clear what it is about predestination that leaves the damned in hell, but insisted that the words of scripture must be taken 'as speaking the truth' and not merely 'as a threat' (*City of God* 22.1–28).

Augustine saw church membership as a supportive and helpful context in which to live a godly life, and from which to pray for and call others to become children of God. When Augustine speaks of the Church, he sometimes means the gathering of the faithful who trace their origins to the apostles, and sometimes the pilgrim people who have lived by faith since Old Testament times. Sometimes he means the blessed company known only to God, who are predestined to immortal bliss. Whatever the image, there is a sense of identity and process in his thought.

The Church

For Augustine, the task of the bishop was to call people into the Church, baptize them and administer communion to them. A bishop was an expression of the unity of the Church and its continuity since the time of the apostles. Apostolic authority was important to Augustine, who looked to Rome as the senior see in the west, probably not least because the apostles Peter and Paul were buried there. On occasion, Rome would be asked to give a ruling on a contentious issue, but as often as not the African bishops decided matters among themselves.

Throughout Augustine's lifetime there were two churches in Africa, the Catholic and the Donatist, each

St Peter's Basilica
and Square in
modern Rome.

with its own bishops and clergy. This raised the question
as to which church was true, who were the true believers,
and whose administration of the sacraments of baptism
and holy communion was effective.

The African Church owed its distinctive identity to
Cyprian. Augustine, particularly through the challenge
of the Donatists, was forced to think again about
what defined the Church in terms of its sacraments,
membership and boundaries. As a result, he noted four
characteristics: unity, holiness, catholicity and apostolicity.
For Augustine, the unity of the Church was to be found in
its communion of faith, administration of the sacraments,

and loving service. To this end he opposed heresy, schism and sin (which was lack of love) as the enemies of the true Church. The authority of the Church was expressed in its Catholic doctrine and councils, and in the 'seat of Peter', which is the primacy of apostolic teaching.

Both Catholics and Donatists had believed that the Holy Spirit was only active in the lives of those who received the sacraments. Augustine argued vigorously that those who were in rebellion against the true Church were outsiders to the faith and no different from pagans and unbaptized infants. In their fallen state, humans have no power to avoid sin, or to will and do good.

Augustine's spirituality

The story of Augustine's spiritual journey is told in his own words in *Confessions*. From the complex mythology and strict asceticism of the Manichees, he discovers a way to God that is not centred on intellect or self-denial, but on love. This is a Christian life that is expressed in actions, motivated by the love of God, which has been revealed for each individual and for the whole world through his Son Jesus Christ. We hear a passion for God in Augustine's reflections and prayers, which indicates a heart open to intimate communion with the divine. Here is someone who delights in God, knowing that he has become a child of God, not by effort, but by God's amazing grace.

It is central to Augustine's spirituality that humans are made in God's image (Genesis 1:26), but an image that has been defaced by sin. It is this 'image' that enables humans to remember, understand and love God. The image of God was marred at the Fall, but the capacity for friendship with God remained. From Plotinus he learned the idea of the inner spiritual journey, first from the exterior world of appearances to the interior world of the soul, and then to the superior realm of the divine. At baptism, the Holy Spirit enters the soul, bestowing his gift of grace and making it the dwelling place of the Trinity. For Augustine, the goal of the spiritual life is to have restored in one's self, and in community, the image of God. This is received by loving God and fellow humans, and by living in harmony and mutual regard.

That all this is the journey of a lifetime is expressed in Augustine's prayer at the end of *On the Trinity*: 'Lord God, Trinity, may I be mindful of you, understand you, love you. Increase these gifts in me until you have entirely reformed me' (15.28.51).

Christ giving
communion to
his apostles.
Russian ikon
(c. 1600).

Augustine differed from Cyprian in believing that
a person who is ordained to the priesthood cannot
subsequently forfeit that ordination or the ability to
administer the sacraments effectively. Augustine drew a
careful distinction in the sacrament between the visible sign
(bread, wine, water), the invisible grace that it represented,
and the benefit enjoyed by the faithful recipient. A
sacrament is always 'valid' wherever it is administered, but
it is 'fruitful' only within the Church. For Augustine, the
effectiveness of the sacrament depended neither entirely on
the faith of the priest administering it nor on the faith of
the person receiving it; but he emphasized the importance
of the Church as the only place where the unity of the Spirit
is to be found. 'Those who do not love the unity of the
Church do not have the charity of God' (*On Baptism* 3.16.21).

Augustine taught that the head of the Church is Christ, who is always present and active in the Church, which is his body. This body has the Holy Spirit as its soul, and as such cannot be divided. From this he argued that the Holy Spirit could not be active outside the Church, and least of all in those who were wilfully in rebellion against it. The visible Church, too, is imperfect, but within it are the saints who are eternally part of the kingdom of God. The Holy Spirit draws all the saints into a community with the faithful people of Israel and the blessed angels in heaven. When all is complete, this will be the kingdom of God in its fullness.

Summary

Although Augustine did not write systematically, his work has proved foundational to Christian thought and practice in every subsequent age. His *Confessions* have informed awareness of the inner life; his engagement with the Donatists shaped the identity and government of the Church; and his doctrine of grace and the elect identified a spiritual conundrum that is with us to this day.

Augustinian
monks at prayer.

Monasticism

From his first experiment at living in community, at Cassiciacum, Augustine never lived alone. On their return to Thagaste, the friends formed a fellowship of 'the servants of God' committed to contemplative philosophy. At Hippo as a bishop he founded a monastery, turning the episcopal house into a clerical monastic community, a nursery that produced many African bishops.

This 'religious' life was a corporate reflection of Augustine's ideal of the whole Church: a witness to the future kingdom of God. The Rule associated with Augustine, and the monastic orders of monks and nuns that bear his name or follow his tradition, emphasizes 'Living in freedom under grace'. It seeks that a monastic community be a microcosm of the city of God, longing for mystical union with God, but also firmly rooted in the love and service of others, both within the community and in the wider world.

There is no mention of Augustine's Rule, in his own *Reconsiderations* or Possidius's *Catalogue*, but there is evidence of a monastic rule attributed to Augustine a century after his death. Benedict of Nursia (c. 480–547) knew of it and was influenced by it, as were several other founders of religious orders. The origins of Augustinian Canons (also known as 'Black', 'Regular' and 'Austin' Canons) are connected with the reform movement of Pope Gregory VII's time (c. 1021–85). Such canons did not belong to a single order but were organized into various houses, which in turn subdivided into congregations. Thomas à Kempis and Gerhard Groote belonged to Windesheim, and Erasmus was an Augustinian Canon. Canons Regular of the Lateran and the Premonstratensian Canons still survive, and two famous teaching hospitals in London, St Bartholomew's and St Thomas's, owe their origins to the Augustinian movement.

Through the ages

Interest in Augustine has been continuous during the 15 centuries since his death. Boethius (480–527) acknowledged 'the seeds sown in my mind by Augustine's writing', while Benedict of Nursia owed much to Augustine's template when drawing up his Rule for western monasticism. Gregory the Great (540–604) put Augustine's principles into practice in both his spirituality and his churchmanship.

The list of Augustine's debtors is long: Anselm and Aquinas among the scholastics, Luther among the reformers, Pascal among the mystics, and Kierkegaard and Wittgenstein among the philosophers, are only a few of the famous names. And Petrarch was never without Augustine, for he carried a copy of the *Confessions* in his pocket.

Some 20,000 books have been written about Augustine, as well as a vast number of scholarly papers and articles. His works are available on disk, and websites are devoted to him. As long as we human beings ponder our own nature, the nature of the divine, and the relationship between the two, Augustine will continue to inspire and instruct.

Chronology

13 November 354: Augustine is born at Thagaste (Souk-Ahras, in Algeria).

361: Attends first school in Thagaste; becomes seriously ill.

366–69: At school in Madauros.

369–70: Returns to Thagaste; has a year of idleness.

370–73: Studies in Carthage; has a mistress.

c. 371: Augustine's father, Patricius, dies.

372: Augustine's son, Adeodatus, is born.

373: Augustine reads Cicero's *Hortensius* and is converted to philosophy; becomes a Manichee.

373–74: Teaches rhetoric in Thagaste.

376: Teaches rhetoric in Carthage.

380–81: Writes first book, *On the Beautiful and the Fitting.*

381: Council of Constantinople.

383: Meets Faustus of Milevis and begins to have doubts about Manichaeism; leaves Carthage and teaches in Rome.

Autumn 384: Appointed official orator in Milan.

Spring 385: Monica arrives in Milan.

Spring 386: Augustine reads some Platonic books and studies Paul's letters.

August 386: Visited by Ponticianus; converts to Christianity.

September 386: Retreats to Cassiciacum; writes the first *Dialogues.*

March 387: Returns to Milan.

Easter 387: Is baptized by Ambrose in Milan on 24 April; shares vision with Monica at Ostia; Monica dies.

387–88: Returns to Rome; begins anti-Manichaean writings.

388: Returns to Africa, to Carthage, then settles in Thagaste and begins monastic life there.

388–90: Adeodatus and Nebridius die.

Spring 391: Augustine begins monastic life in Hippo and is ordained priest there (Hippo Regius, Annaba, in Algeria).

392: Debate in Hippo with Fortunatus; Augustine begins writing the *Explanations of the Psalms.*

October 393: Speaks at Council of Hippo.

June 394: Council of Carthage.

395: Consecrated bishop of Hippo.

396: Rereads Paul; develops theology of grace.

June and August 397: Takes part at Councils of Carthage; preaching campaign at Carthage; begins writing the *Confessions.*

April 399: Council of Carthage; begins writing *On the Trinity.*

June and September 401: Councils of Carthage.

August 402: Attends Council of Milevis.

August 403: Council of Carthage; preaches regularly at Carthage.

June 404: Council of Carthage.

August 405: Council of Carthage.

406: Begins writing *Tractates on the Gospel of John.*

June 407: Council of Thubursicum.

June and October 408: Councils of Carthage.

June 409: Council of Carthage.

410: Alaric enters Rome.

May–September 410: Visits to Carthage.

June 410: Council of Carthage.

Winter 410: Retreats to villa outside Hippo because of ill health.

411: Preaches regularly in Carthage and Cirta against the Donatists.

June 411: Plays a decisive role in the Assembly (*Collatio*) debate between Catholics and Donatists; beginning of debate with the Pelagians; develops doctrine of original sin.

411–12: Has connections with aristocratic refugees from the sack of Rome.

412: Begins writing the *City of God* (completed in 427).

June 412: Synod at Cirta; preaches regularly in Carthage.

413: Fails to prevent the execution of Flavius Marcellinus at Carthage.

September and October 416: Attends the Councils of Milevis.

September 417: Preaches at Carthage.

May 418: Council of Carthage.

September 418: Augustine at Caesarea in Mauretania.

May 419: Council of Carthage; debate with Julian of Eclanum begins.

June 421: Council of Carthage.

426: Augustine visits Milevis, leaves Hippo; again suffers from poor health; begins *Reconsiderations*.

428: Debate with Maximus at Hippo.

429–30: Vandals enter Africa and lay siege to Hippo.

28 August 430: Augustine dies in Hippo.

Suggestions for Further Reading

Gerald Bonner, *St Augustine of Hippo: Life and Controversies*, London: SCM Press, 1963, rev. ed. Norwich: Canterbury Press, 1986.

Peter Brown, *Augustine of Hippo: A Biography*, London: Faber, 1967, rev. ed. 2000.

Averil Cameron, *The Later Roman Empire*, London: Fontana, 1993.

Henry Chadwick, *Augustine*, Oxford: Oxford University Press, 1986.

Henry Chadwick, *Augustine: A Very Short Introduction*, Oxford: Oxford University Press, 2001.

Mary T. Clark, *Augustine*, London: Geoffrey Chapman, 1994.

Allan D. Fitzgerald O.S.A. (general editor), *Augustine through the Ages: An Encyclopedia*, Grand Rapids and Cambridge: Eerdmans, 1999.

Carol Harrison, *Augustine: Christian Truth and Fractured Humanity*, Oxford: Oxford University Press, 2000.

Serge Lancel, *St Augustine*, Paris: Fayard, 1999, English translation: Antonia Nevill, London: SCM Press, 2002.

Robert A. Markus, *Saeculum: History and Society in the Theology of St Augustine*, Cambridge: Cambridge University Press, 1970, rev. ed. 1989.

James J. O'Donnell, *Augustine: Conferences*, 3 volumes, Oxford: Oxford University Press, 1992.

John J. O'Meara, *The Young Augustine: The Growth of St Augustine's Mind up to His Conversion*, London: Longmans, 1954, rev. ed. 1980.

Paul Monceaux, *Histoire litteraire de l'Afrique chrétienne*, Brussels, 1966.

Richard Price, *Augustine*, London: HarperCollins, 1996.

John Rist, *Augustine*, Cambridge: Cambridge University Press, 1994.

Colin Wells, *The Roman Empire*, London: Fontana, 1992.

Garry Wills, *St Augustine*, London: Orion, 2000.

Websites

James J. O'Donnell's website at: www.georgetown.edu/faculty/jod/augustine

Index

Picture and Text Acknowledgments

Pictures

Picture research by Zooid Pictures Limited.

AKG – Images: pp. 20, 23, 52, 64, 79, 83, 140–41, 158, 160; 2–3 (Gilles Mermet); 38–39, 98 (Erich Lessing); 112 (Jean-Louis Nou); 145, 164 (British Library).

Bridgeman Art Library: pp. 14–15 (Bibliothèque des Arts Decoratifs, Paris, France), 33 (Bibliothèque Nationale, Paris, France), 34 (Museo Episcopal de Vic, Osona, Catalonia, Spain/Index), 59 (Bibliothèque Municipale, Avranches, France), 72–73 (Musee d'Art Thomas Henry, Cherbourg, France), 129, 132 (Bibliothèque Municipale, Dijon, France), 139 (Bibliothèque Municipale, Arras, France), 148–49 (New York Historical Society, New York, USA), 153 (British Museum, London, UK), 162–63 (Topkapi Palace Museum, Istanbul, Turkey).

Corbis UK Ltd.: pp. 12–13, 80–81, 170–71; 1 (North Carolina Museum of Art); 4 (Elio Ciol); 16 (Jonathan Blair); 17 (CRD Photo); 19 (Mimmo Jodice); 26–27 (Christine Osborne); 31 (National Gallery Collection; By kind permission of the Trustees of the National Gallery, London); 49, 68 (Araldo de Luca); 56, 108–109, 124 (Archivo Iconografico, S.A.); 62–63 (Angelo Hornak); 92–93 (Roger Wood); 104 (Charles and Josette Lenars); 120–21 (Dean Conger); 134–35, 159 (Chris Hellier); 147 (Bettmann); 174–75 (Mark L. Stephenson); 178 (James L. Amos).

Hulton|Archive/Getty Images: p. 122.

Mary Evans Picture Library: p. 96.

Scala Art Resource: pp. 84, 156; 67, 103, 154–55 (Courtesy of the Ministero Beni e Att. Culturali).

Text

For sources of Augustine's works see the Introduction and Suggestions for Further Reading.

Lion Publishing

Commissioning editor: Morag Reeve

Project editors: Jenni Dutton, Laura Derico

Designer: Nicholas Rous

Production manager: Kylie Ord